The Diviners: A Play

The Diviners: A Play

Based on the novel
by Margaret Laurence

Text by Vern Thiessen
with Yvette Nolan

SCIROCCO DRAMA

The Diviners
first published 2024 by Scirocco Drama
An imprint of J. Gordon Shillingford Publishing Inc.
© 2024 Vern Thiessen with Yvette Nolan

Scirocco Drama Editor: Glenda MacFarlane
Cover design by Doowah Design

Author photo of Vern Thiessen by Warren Sulatycky
Author photo of Yvette Nolan by Redworks
Author photo of Margaret Laurence by Doug Boult

Michif translations by Lorraine Coutu
French translations by Lorraine Forbes

Production inquiries
Michael Petrasek, Kensington Literary
kensingtonlit@rogers.com

Library and Archives Canada Cataloguing in Publication
Title: The diviners : a play : based on the novel by Margaret Laurence / text by
Vern Thiessen with Yvette Nolan.
Names: Thiessen, Vern, author. | Nolan, Yvette, contributor. | Adaptation of
(work): Laurence, Margaret. Diviners.
Identifiers: Canadiana 20240455118 | ISBN 9781990738593 (softcover)
Subjects: LCGFT: Drama.
Classification: LCC PS8589.H4524 D58 2024 | DDC C812/.54—dc23

We acknowledge the financial support of the Canada Council for the Arts,
the Government of Canada, the Manitoba Arts Council, and the Manitoba
Government for our publishing program.

J. Gordon Shillingford Publishing
P.O. Box 86, RPO Corydon Avenue, Winnipeg, MB Canada R3M 3S3

Vern Thiessen

Vern Thiessen is one of Canada's most produced playwrights. His plays have been seen across Canada, the UK, United States, Europe, Australia, New Zealand, and Asia and have been translated into five languages. His works include *Of Human Bondage, Vimy, Einstein's Gift* (Governor General's Literary Award winner), *Lenin's Embalmers* (Governor General's Literary Award finalist), *Apple,* and *Shakespeare's Will*. He has been produced off-Broadway five times. Vern is the recipient of numerous awards, including the Dora Mavor Moore and Sterling awards for Outstanding New Play, The Carol Bolt Award, the Gwen Pharis Ringwood Award, the City of Edmonton Arts Achievement Award, the University of Alberta Alumni Award of Excellence, the Canadian Jewish Playwriting Competition, and the Governor General's Literary Award for Drama, Canada's highest honour for a playwright. He was also a finalist for the Siminovitch Prize in Playwriting. Vern received his B.A. from the University of Winnipeg and an M.F.A. from the University of Alberta. He has served as president of both the Playwrights Guild of Canada and the Writers Guild of Alberta. For six years he served as Artistic Director of Workshop West Playwrights Theatre, one of Canada's leading new play companies. He is married to acclaimed screenwriter and novelist Susie Moloney.

Yvette Nolan

Yvette Nolan (Algonquin) is a playwright, director and dramaturg. Her works include the plays *The Unplugging*, *The Art of War*, *Annie Mae's Movement*, *The Birds (a modern adaptation of Aristophanes' comedy)*, the dance-opera Bearing, the libretto *Shawnadithit*, the short play-for-film *Katharsis*, and the virtual reality piece *Reconciling* for Boca del Lupo. She co-created, with Joel Bernbaum and Lancelot Knight, the verbatim play *Reasonable Doubt*, about relations between Indigenous and non-Indigenous communities in Saskatchewan. From 2003 to 2011, she served as the Artistic Director of Native Earth Performing Arts. Her book, *Medicine Shows*, about Indigenous performance in Canada, was published by Playwrights Canada Press in 2015, and *Performing Indigeneity* (co-edited with Ric Knowles) in 2016. Born in Prince Albert, raised in Winnipeg, Yvette has lived all over this land, from Nova Scotia to the Yukon.

Margaret Laurence

Jean Margaret Laurence was a Canadian novelist and short story writer and is one of the major figures in Canadian literature. She was also a founder of the Writers' Union of Canada and Writers' Trust of Canada, a non-profit literary organization.

One of Canada's most esteemed and beloved authors by the end of her literary career, Laurence began writing short stories in her teenage years while in Neepawa, Manitoba. Her first published piece "The Land of Our Father" was submitted to a competition held by the *Winnipeg Free Press*. This story contains the first appearance of the name "Manawaka" (a fictional Canadian town used in many of her later works).

It was after her return to Canada from West Africa that she wrote *The Stone Angel* (1964), the novel for which she is best known. The novel was for a time required reading in many North American school systems and colleges. Laurence was published by the Canadian publishing company McClelland & Stewart, and she became one of the key figures in the emerging Canadian literary tradition.

Rachel, Rachel is a 1968 film directed by Paul Newman based on Laurence's novel *A Jest of God*. *The Stone Angel*, a feature-length film based on Laurence's novel, written and directed by Kari Skogland and starring Ellen Burstyn, premiered in 2007.

Laurence won two Governor General's Awards for her novels *A Jest of God* (1966) and *The Diviners* (1974). In 1972 she was invested as a Companion of the Order of Canada. In 2016 she was named a National Historic Person.

Acknowledgements

Thanks to Krista Jackson, Geneviève Pelletier, and Andrina Turenne for their critical collaboration on this project. Thanks to Elder Delorès Gosselin for her blessing and leadership. Thanks to the Estate of Margaret Laurence for allowing us to create this work. Thanks to all the amazing artists who have been part of the development process on this project.

Playwrights' Note

Margaret Laurence's novel *The Diviners* has been called epic, a *künstlerroman*, powerful—a classic. On her way to becoming the writer she will be, the author of this epic story within a story, Morag Gunn, deals with her past, with race, class, poverty, violence, sex and sexuality, abortion, loneliness, single motherhood, love and honour, guilt and shame, and aging. She is swamped by memories, looking backward in order to figure out how to move forward. *The Diviners* is, for us, a play about reconciliation. The story of the Tonnerres—Jules, Lazarus and Piquette—is inextricably interwoven with Morag's story. In order to heal and become the writer she will be, Morag must grapple with the history of the place where she lives and open her heart to know the truth of the family who lives on the outskirts of Manawaka. Margaret Laurence brought the Tonnerres to life in *The Diviners*. The way the novel moves forward and backward in time — Morag's "memorybank" movies, crashing into her present-day life in her log cabin near McConnell's Landing, crashing into the actual act of writing, the inclusion of the songs—lends itself to adaptation for the stage.

Theatre is a collaborative art, and the process of bringing *The Diviners* to the stage has been a steadfast model of that collaboration. The text has been influenced by every artist, every elder and every knowledge keeper who came into contact with it, from the earliest workshops in Winnipeg to the rehearsal hall at Stratford. The actors' voices speaking the lines into the air informed us as writers how to weave this story together. We wrote and rewrote, tweaked and zhuzhed, changing a line here, moving a few lines from there, always in conversation with our incredible collaborators and all their artistry in service of this play; this telling of this story, imagined into being over fifty years ago, reimagined today in an effort to understand how we live together better, here, now and moving forward. Margaret Laurence created these characters on the page; we hope that we are able to bring them to life in a theatrical form so that we can hear them sing, see them struggle and understand that their story is our story, and our story is about recognizing that we are all connected.

Yvette Nolan and Vern Thiessen

Foreword

by Keith Barker

Number 83 of the 94 Calls to Action from the Truth and Reconciliation Commission calls upon the Canada Council for the Arts, our federal arts funder, to prioritize funding to undertake collaborative projects and produce works that contribute to the reconciliation process. If you are unfamiliar with what I am referring to, please Google it. It is essential reading.

The adaptation of *The Diviners* from the novel to the play embodies the essence of Call #83. Here is what I believe makes this play so special:

Two of Canada's most prolific playwrights collaborated on the play: one is Algonquin, one is a Settler. The other two co-creators directed the premiere production at the Stratford Festival. One director is Métis—nothing about us without us—one director is a Ukrainian-mixed-European Canadian. All four of the creators grew up on Treaty One Territory, where the book and the eventual play is based, which is also the home of Manitoba's first premier, and the "OG" of the Métis people, Louis Riel. The designers on this production were a mix of Indigenous and non-Indigenous artists (highly recommend this for future productions, just saying). The company of actors in this production—also a mix of Indigenous and non-Indigenous artists. The two elders on this production: one was Métis from Treaty One Territory, and the other was from Kettle & Stony Point First Nation, the territory that hosted the production, and the land the Stratford Festival calls home.

The Commission thoughtfully recognized that projects like these require people to be in a room together for many, MANY days—which, by its nature, requires consistent communication, and demands that people be in relation with one another.

On the first day of rehearsals, we talked about a value-based approach to the work—what values did the company want to uphold in the room? Because making theatre is hard. The creation process is rife with opportunities for misunderstanding, competing interests, and hurt feelings, which is complicated further by artists working to the edge of their capacity, in service of the play. It also has the potential for epiphanies and breakthroughs, comradery, integrity, joy, laughter, and compromise. All these things are true at once, and right relations require patience, humility, empathy, wisdom, courage, tolerance, and strength of character. They are aspirational, of course, difficult to hold all at once, but we learn in the trying.

The Diviners explores the life of Morag Gunn, a fiercely independent forty-seven-year-old single mother and writer. Morag has to navigate complex relationships with her daughter and lover. The story shifts between her present life, and her past, delving into her childhood, her relationships, and her struggles with identity. The novel tackles controversial issues, including poverty, race, sexuality, class and abortion, all quite daring for 1974. In challenging societal norms, several attempts were made to ban the book. In terms of censorship in Canada, *The Diviners* stands out as one of the pivotal literary controversies of the twentieth century.

I first read *The Diviners* in high school, which is saying a lot, because I was never really a good student. This book was the exception; it was the first time I had experienced a Métis narrative within a story. I remember thinking the book felt like a movie; it was easy to read, like Margaret was speaking to me directly.

I had that same feeling the first time I read the play. It captured so much of what I had loved in the novel, with a new take that centred the Métis story, exposing the messy and complicated history of settlement in this new country called Canada.

The play, like the book, reminds us that time is cyclical, by beginning and ending with the river that flows both ways, much like the past is the future and the future is the past.

It is a reminder that despite all the places we have come from, and all the places that we have landed, we are, all of us, related.

Enjoy.

Keith Barker is the director of the Forester Bernstein New Play Development Program at the Stratford Festival.

Production History

The Diviners was originally produced by the Stratford Festival, Ontario, Canada. The World Premiere production opened on August 24, 2024 at the Tom Patterson Theatre. Antoni Cimolino, Artistic Director, and Anita Gaffney, Executive Director.

Cast *(in alphabetical order)*

Lachlan	Christopher Allen
Gord, Piper Gunn	Gabriel Antonacci
Brooke	Dan Chameroy
Piquette	Caleigh Crow
Crispin	Allison Edwards-Crewe
Jules	Jesse Gervais
Christie	Jonathan Goad
Lazarus	Josue Laboucane
Pique, Young Pique, Scots Morag	Julie Lumsden
Morag	Irene Poole
Royland	Anthony Santiago
Gus	Tyrone Savage
Eva, Duchess	Sara Topham

Ensemble :
Michelle Bardach, Carla Bennett, Jarret Cody, Bethany Kovarik, Gracie Mack, Jordan Mah, Chris Mejaki, Evan Mercer, Olivia Sinclair-Brisbane

Onstage Musician:
The Métis Fiddler .... Darla Daniels

Artistic Team

Director .... Krista Jackson with
Geneviève Pelletier

Choreographer................................... Cameron Carver

Set and Lighting Designer.................... Bretta Gerecke

Costume Designer .... Jeff Chief

Composer.. Andrina Turenne

Music Director and Arranger.............. MJ Dandeneau

Additional Composition and
Sound Designer................................... MJ Dandeneau

Dramaturgs.. Krista Jackson,
Yvette Nolan

Fight and Intimacy Director................... Anita Nittoly

Métis Cultural Consultant........... Geneviève Pelletier

Cultural and Praxis Consultant.......Dolorès Gosselin

Cultural Consultant................................Yvette Nolan

French and Michif Language
Consultant .... Lina Le Gal

Jigging Consultant................................ Darla Daniels

Voice, Text and Dialect Coach.......... Jane Gooderham

Executive Producer ....David Auster

Casting Directors ....Beth Russell,
Ari Weinberg

Creative Planning Director...................... Jason Miller

Director of the Foerster Bernstein
New Play Development Program .... Keith Barker

Production Team

Stage Manager...Kelly Luft

Assistant Stage Managers....Jordan Guetter, Suzanne
McArthur, Melissa Rood

Assistant Choreographer....................... Gracie Mack

Assistant Set and Costume Designer........ Ariel Slack

Assistant Lighting Designer................Simran Kapoor

Dance Captain.. Gracie Mack

Fight Captain and Intimacy
Captain..Julie Lumsden

Vocal Captain .... Jarret Cody

Production Stage Managers ....Meghan Callan,
                                                        Elizabeth McDermott

Production Assistant .... Abby Stevenson

Technical Director...............................Greg Dougherty

Development History
This play was developed by Théâtre Cercle Molière with
the assistance of a Manitoba Arts Council ADAPT grant.
An earlier version of this play was commissioned by the
Royal Manitoba Theatre Centre. Further development by
the Stratford Festival of Canada.

Translations
Michif translation by Lorraine Coutu. French translation
by Lorraine Forbes.

Characters

MORAG .... A novelist

PIQUE .... Morag and Jules's daughter

JULES .... A singer / songwriter,
childhood friend,
and lover to Morag

CHRISTIE .... Morag's guardian / adopted father

LAZARUS .... Jules's father

ROYLAND .... Morag's neighbour

GORD .... Pique's boyfriend

LACHLAN .... Morag's boss at a
community newspaper

EVA .... Morag's childhood friend

GUS .... Eva's father

BROOKE .... Morag's ex-husband

CRISPIN .... Morag's agent

PIQUETTE .... Jules's sister / Lazarus's daughter

OTHERS .... as we encounter them.

Time

Time flows seamlessly between past, present, and future. The present of this world is the mid-1970s. We travel as far back as the mid 1930s. We travel into the future to the here and now.

Setting

We float through the settings of this play like a canoe on a river: effortless; simple; surprising, and sometimes startling.

Music

The fiddle. The drum. The pipes. All lyrics here are written by Margaret Laurence, and are part of the copyright of the novel with the exception of "Falcon's Song" which is in the public domain. In some cases lyrics were adapted by Andrina Turenne. "Faiye dedo peanutte" was found online with no credit listed. We believe it is traditional.

Style

The company members rarely leave the stage. They are Morag's words, her imagination, her memory. They may speak individually or as a group. If characters appear they are in front of us, and not a voice-over.

Act One

A river — like a Métis sash.

MORAG at her typewriter.

PIQUE with a knapsack.

ROYLAND with fishing gear.

PIQUETTE in a bright red coat.

The other company members watch.

ROYLAND: Morag, what's wrong?

MORAG: Pique — she's left!

PIQUE: You want me to "do something with my life," you got it.

ROYLAND: What happened?

MORAG: We had a fight.

PIQUE: You been making decisions for me my whole life.

MORAG: I'm your mother. It's my job to protect you.

PIQUE: From what?

PIQUE/
PIQUETTE: From WHAT?

MORAG: ...Pique.

PIQUE: Ya see? You can't even say it. Goodbye, Ma.

MORAG:	Wait! At least tell me where you're going.
PIQUE/ PIQUETTE:	West.
MORAG:	West?
PIQUE:	There's things I gotta see for myself.
MORAG:	But you don't have a car, how are you—?
PIQUE:	I'll hitchhike.
MORAG:	Alone?
PIQUE:	I gotta go. I can't do this with you anymore.
ROYLAND:	Oh boy. What about Gord?

PIQUE turns:

PIQUE:	And if Gord shows any concern, tell him I've drowned and gone floating down the river, crowned with algae and dead minnows, like Ophelia.

She leaves.

ROYLAND:	Well, you gotta give the girl marks for style.
MORAG:	It's not funny, Royland.
ROYLAND:	Never said it was.
MORAG:	She's eighteen!
ROYLAND:	She'll be fine.
MORAG:	This isn't the 60s where you could hitchhike across the country and never get murdered.
ROYLAND:	She knows how to take care of herself. You taught her that.
MORAG:	I've never been able to teach that girl anything.

ROYLAND: How old were you when you left home, Morag?

MORAG: That was different. I was going to university.

ROYLAND: Maybe a log cabin in the Ontario bush isn't enough for her.

PIQUETTE: City is hard.

MORAG: It's 1972. We've got Charles Manson and Bedroom Stranglers...

PIQUETTE: Maybe she'll find herself a nice white fella, Morag.

MORAG: And west! Toronto, I can see. But west?

ROYLAND: What's out west anyway?

MORAG looks at PIQUETTE.

MORAG: Too much, is what.

PIQUETTE vanishes.

ROYLAND: Huh. She'll be back before you know it.

MORAG: What am I going to do, Royland?

ROYLAND: Let me talk to Gord.

MORAG: Thanks.

ROYLAND: I'm taking him over to Charlie Green's today. I'll let him know.

MORAG: Why Charlie Green?

ROYLAND: Divine a well, eventually. Wanna come?

MORAG: I need to work.

ROYLAND: If I had a nickel for every time you told me you were gonna start that new book.

MORAG: It's not easy, ya know. You don't just sit down and write a novel.

ROYLAND: I suppose not. But eventually, the fish needs to get caught. Here.

                        He slaps down a live fish on her writing desk.

                        Muskie. Straight from the river. Fry it in butter. It's best that way.

MORAG: *(Slightly disgusted.)* Thanks.

ROYLAND: I'm heading into McConnell's Landing. Need anything?

MORAG: A bottle of Scotch.

ROYLAND: Just one?

                        She shoots him a look.

MORAG: Where do you get it?

ROYLAND: What?

MORAG: All this...*wis-dom*.

ROYLAND: Same place I caught that fish. All kinds of ways to divine in this world, Morag.

                        He leaves.

                                    ***

                        MORAG sits down at the typewriter.

                        She rolls in a piece of paper.

                        Stares at it.

MORAG: I can't...

CHRISTIE: Morag.

EVA: Write it.

PIQUETTE: It's time.

She stares out.

She starts to type.

This need not be realistic.

But like a real typewriter, it should be physical and noisy, and complicated, like she is playing an ancient instrument or constructing a building or hammering a nail with every word.

CHRISTIE: The River.

She stops. She types again.

JULES: *(French.) La Rivière.*

LAZARUS: *(Michif.) La Rivyayr.*

MORAG takes a deep breath.

She types again.

MORAG: The river flows both ways.

ENSEMBLE: The river flows both ways.

Her memory flows as do her fingers.

                        ***

A train station. CHRISTIE LOGAN, hat in his hands.

CHRISTIE: Morag Gunn?

She nods, shy and terrified.   He too, is terrified.

(A faded Scottish brogue.) I'm Christie Logan. Did they not send you with any suitcase, lass?

She shakes her head.

All right, then. Come with me.

They travel. Or perhaps, the world travels past them.

MORAG: Mr. Logan...

CHRISTIE: None of that. You'll call me Christie.

MORAG: What happened to my parents?

CHRISTIE: Did they not tell you, girl?

She shakes her head.

Fools. Think children can't handle the truth. It was the polio, got them both. You know what that is?

MORAG nods.

They didn't have no other relatives so... You'll stay with me till your schooling's done. It was me or the orphanage in Winnipeg. And they figured here in Manawaka was better.

My wife Prin, she died last year. Got no children of my own. I promise I'll do my best.

You'll like living in town. Once you get used to it.

***

A bell rings.

KID: Look! It's Old Man Logan!

KID: Rag Picker!

KID: Pee-you! You can smell him from here!

KIDS: Christie Logan's the Scavenger Man —
                Gets his food from the garbage can!

                *CHRISTIE acts the crazy fool. It scares
                them.*

CHRISTIE: Seen enough?!

                *They run off. He takes MORAG by her
                shoulders.*

                Now listen here, Morag. Don't you take
                any smart-aleck stuff from any of that lot,
                there. They're only muck the same as any of
                us. Skin and bone and the odd bit of guts.
                Understand?

                            ***

                A bell.

KID: Lookit her!

KID: Her dress!

KID: It's down to her ankles!

KIDS: Mo-rag! Mo-rag!
                Gets her clothes from an ol' flour bag!

                They laugh.

TEACHER: *(An angel.)* Welcome, boys and girls. I know
                you're going to work hard and not make any
                trouble, is that correct?

KIDS: Yes, Miss Crawford.

KID: CrawFISH!

                They laugh hysterically.

TEACHER slaps the ruler violently.

TEACHER: *(A demon.)* Silence! Any troublemakers will find themselves with a ruler across the hands.

Silence.

Now if you need to leave the room, you must put up your finger, either one or two, if you take my meaning.

KID: *(Whispers to another.)* If you gotta do Number Two, she lets you go out right away.

She slaps the ruler down.

TEACHER: *All stand!* We will now sing "God Save the King."

All the kids rise except JULES TONNERRE.

The TEACHER leads, and they sing.

"God Save our Gracious King. Long—"

Wait. Skinner Tonnerre! Stand and sing.

He does not.

I've heard you, Skinner. Singing those songs you people sing. You have a good voice.

KID: Dumb half-breed.

KID: Stupid Indian.

KID: Métis, get it right!

TEACHER: Sing "God Save the King" or I will give you the ruler!

JULES: He's not my king!

KIDS: *(Apoplectic.)* Ooooo…. Ohhhh.

TEACHER: Skinner Tonnerre, come here right now!

                He does. He lays his hand out. The
                TEACHER brings up the ruler.

MORAG: Stop!

TEACHER: What?

MORAG: It's not right!

TEACHER: Morag Gunn, you be quiet.

MORAG: Don't hit him!

TEACHER: Come here, Morag! You will *both* get the ruler!

KID: Oooh, what's that smell!

                They step away, to reveal EVA WINKLER,
                standing and crying. She wears a standard
                Mennonite shawl and dress.

TEACHER: Eva Winkler!

KID: She's pooped her pants!

TEACHER: Silence! Eva, why didn't you ask permission,
                like I told you?

EVA: I couldn't, I couldn't—

TEACHER: Morag, help Eva to the washroom. And you,
                Skinner, go get the janitor. Now, let us sing!

MORAG: It's okay, Eva.

EVA: She was going to hit you both. It's no good
                being hit like that. It's no good.

                She bursts into tears and runs off.

JULES: Hey, Morag.

MORAG: Yeh?

JULES: Thanks, eh.

                A moment passes between them. It exists in
                the past, present, and future.

                        ***

                The school bell rings. And the phone rings.

                MORAG is typing madly, but the
                distraction ends up on the page:

CHRISTIE: Aren't ya gonna get that?

MORAG: Shh!

EVA: It could be me calling.

MORAG: Can't you see I'm—!

PIQUE: Or me, Ma.

MORAG: *(Realizing.)* Oh my God.

CHRISTIE: *Answer the christly phone!*

                        ***

MORAG: Pique? Is that you?

JULES: Morag.

MORAG: Who is this?

JULES: Don't recognize me no more, eh?

                JULES is there in the room, as all the
                characters on the phone are.

MORAG: Skinner? Are you all right?

JULES: 'Course I'm all right. You?

MORAG: Same.

JULES: How's Pique?

MORAG:	Oh, Skinner. She's left.
JULES:	Whaddya mean?
MORAG:	She's headed west. Hitchhiking.
JULES:	*(Pleased.)* West, ya say? And you let her go?
MORAG:	What was I supposed to do, chain her to the stove?
JULES:	She had to leave sometime, Morag. Has she got my number?
MORAG:	I don't know.
JULES:	Give it to her when you talk to her next, will ya?

GORD bursts in.

MORAG:	Why?
GORD:	Is it true?

JULES fingers a brooch.

JULES:	I have something for her.
MORAG:	What?
GORD:	What Royland told me?
JULES/ PIQUETTE:	There are things she needs to know.
GORD:	Morag?
MORAG:	I gotta go, Skinner.
JULES:	Hey Morag, say my name. My real name, the way you used to.
MORAG:	Another time.
JULES:	Right. I'll be seein' ya, Morag.

GORD:	*Is it?*
MORAG:	Yes, Gord, it's true.

> *GORD throws himself onto her table/ desk, blubbering. MORAG makes a feeble attempt at comfort.*

	Now, now, Gord.
GORD:	*What will I do without Pique!?*

> *More blubbering.*

MORAG:	She'll be back before you know it.
GORD:	Why, Morag? Without even a goodbye? All I wanted was to spend the rest of my life with her. What's she want from me?
MORAG:	Look, Gord, she cares about you. But she probably wants to be on her own awhile.
GORD:	What can I do? Tell me!
MORAG:	Just be patient. *(Lying.)* All will be fine. I'm sure of it.
GORD:	*(Recovering.)* Well... thanks.

> *He gets up to go.*

GORD:	Royland says you're starting a new book?

> *CHRISTIE appears.*

MORAG:	*(Not convinced.)* Trying.
CHRISTIE:	Here, Morag. Look at this.
GORD:	Well... Happy writing!

> *GORD goes. CHRISTIE is there with a photo.*

Perhaps the shadows of WWI soldiers, posing.

***

CHRISTIE: Put your glasses on, lass.

MORAG: Which one's my father, Christie?

CHRISTIE takes sip of a drink in a mug.

CHRISTIE: There. Corporal Colin Gunn. And there's me. Wouldn't recognize me, would ya?

MORAG: You both look... happy.

CHRISTIE: Aye. Christ knows why. The things we went through.

MORAG: Tell me.

Perhaps we see shadows of this.

CHRISTIE: Your da and me was both gunners. He was my mate, you see. We worked the big gun together.

MORAG: Gunner Gunn. That's neat.

CHRISTIE: Bourlon Wood. September 27. Nineteen Hundred and Eighteen. There we are, getting ready to fire old Brimstone, and a shell explodes so christly close to me I think I'm a goner. And then the air around me, filled with...

MORAG: What?

CHRISTIE: Bleeding bits of a man. A leg. A hand.

MORAG: Oh.

CHRISTIE: I started to shake, see. Couldn't move my feet. Passed out. When I come to, your da gives me some water. He'd dragged me into the dugouts, out of the fire. Saved me, he did. Your father.

She is taking notes.

What're you doing?

MORAG: Writing it down.

CHRISTIE: Why?

MORAG: So I won't forget.

CHRISTIE's hands shake.

CHRISTIE: Screaming. Drowning in mud. Jesus—

MORAG: Christie, are you okay?

CHRISTIE: Aye, he saved me, your father did.

MORAG is typing this out.

MORAG: *(Under her breath.)* "Saved me, your father did."

***

MORAG types, throws back the carriage — ding.

Rips it out. Rips it up. Trashes it. Repeat.

What am I doing, what am I doing, what am I—

ROYLAND: Talking to yourself again, Morag?

MORAG: *(Startled, then.)* Ah! Oh. Yeh. Tools of the trade: Staring at pictures and talking to myself.

ROYLAND: Started, have ya?

MORAG:	Dipping my toe in.
ROYLAND:	And? How's the water?
MORAG:	Ice cold.
ROYLAND:	This'll warm you up. *(The bag.)*
MORAG:	Much needed. What do I owe you?
ROYLAND:	Sharing it. *(He takes it out, opens it.)*
MORAG:	Done.

He pours.

ROYLAND:	*(Cheers.)* Down the hatch.
MORAG:	*(Cheers.)* Fill your boots.

They take the shot and pour another.

MORAG:	I feel like I'm fighting the current.
ROYLAND:	Maybe you shouldn't resist.

CHRISTIE appears on the stoop with a coffee mug.

MORAG: Do you think we can change the past, Royland?

ROYLAND: Truth is… We all change our own past. When it suits us.

***

MORAG approaches with the bottle, pours into CHRISTIE's mug.

CHRISTIE: *(Cheers.)* Fill your boots.

She sits down next to him, writes in her journal.

What're ya writing now?

MORAG:	Nothing. Stories.
CHRISTIE:	Stories are not nothing, Morag.
MORAG:	Christie, who are my ancestors?
CHRISTIE:	Why, you are from the great Clan Gunn is where you are from. Do they teach you nothing at that school?
MORAG:	How would *they* know where *I'm* from?
CHRISTIE:	Because everyone in Manawaka knows it was the Scots made this place what it is.
MORAG:	But *I* don't know!
CHRISTIE:	Then I will *tell* ya.

The company members bring the story to life. They tell the story to MORAG. Perhaps she writes some of it down in her journal.

NOTE: For practical purposes, the characters listed in these "Ancestor Sequences" are only there to reference the actors playing those roles. The characters themselves are not in these scenes.

CHRISTIE:	It was in the old days...
EVA:	...in Scotland
LACHLAN:	In the Suther-lands...
CHRISTIE:	After the battle on the moors...
LAZARUS:	And the clans were broken and scattered...
CRISPIN:	And the dead men thrown into long graves there.
MORAG:	*(Enraptured.)* ...Whoa....

DUCHESS/ EVA:	In those days, there was a Bitch-Duchess.
MORAG:	Whaddya mean?
CHRISTIE:	The Bitch-Duchess ruled the land and its people. But her heart was dark as the feathers of a raven.
DUCHESS/ EVA:	Go! Drive them onto the wild rocks of the shore! We will use these Suther-lands to raise sheep. For sheep pay better than these peasant fools.
CHRISTIE:	And so the people fled. (Go on, flee!)
ACTOR:	Driven to the ends of the land.
LAZARUS:	Where they lived wild on the stormy rocks of the coast.
MORAG:	What happened to them? The Suther-landers?
CHRISTIE:	Well, you see now, Morag, among these people was a man named Piper Gunn.
MORAG:	(Mystical.) Piper Gunn.
ENSEMBLE:	Piper Gunn!
CHRISTIE:	Your ancestor, from the clan Gunn.
LACHLAN:	And Piper Gunn was a great tall man…
LAZARUS:	With the voice of a drum…
ACTOR:	And the heart of a child…
CRISPIN:	And the strength of conviction.
CHRISTIE:	And when he played his pipes…
LAZARUS:	It would wrench the heart of any person not dead as stone.

CHRISTIE: And Piper wore the tartan of his clan, with a great brooch that had the motto of the Gunns on it:

ENSEMBLE: My Hope Is Constant in Thee!

CHRISTIE: And one day, as the people scavenged for food on the barren rocks, Piper Gunn comes to them and says:

PIPER: Dolts and draggards and gutless gutted herring! Why do you sit on these rocks, weeping? For there is a ship coming on the wings of the morning, and we must gather our pots and kettles and shawls and go with this ship into a New World across the waters.

LAZARUS: And the people believed Piper Gunn.

LACHLAN: And began making ready to sail into this New World.

SCOTS MORAG/
PIQUE: Now Piper Gunn had a woman.

CHRISTIE: And a strapping strong woman she was.

ACTOR: With the courage of a falcon…

ACTOR: And the beauty of a deer…

LAZARUS: And the faith of saints.

CHRISTIE: And you may know her name, for it was…

ENSEMBLE: Morag.

MORAG: It was not!

ENSEMBLE: It was!

EVA: And they say…

CHRISTIE: She had the power of second sight.

MORAG: What's that mean, "second sight"?

SCOTS MORAG/
PIQUE: She could see things other people could not. She could feel things other people could not. And she could divine things about other people that they themselves could not.

MORAG: "Second Sight."

ACTOR: As all the people watched that ship come into the harbour.

CAPTAIN/
LAZARUS: Everyone aboard!

CHRISTIE: And when the plank was down, Morag says to her man:

SCOTS MORAG/
PIQUE: Play, Piper Gunn.

CHRISTIE: And what happened then, to all of them people there, homeless on the rocks?

MORAG: What?

SCOTS MORAG/
PIQUE: They rose and followed.

ENSEMBLE: They rose and followed!

CHRISTIE: For Piper Gunn's music put courage into them. Aye, they would have followed him all the way to hell. Which they did.

                The company members leave, following the piper.

MORAG: Whaddya mean, hell?

CHRISTIE: They ended up at the Red River, that's what. In the hell we now call "Winnipeg."

                The phone rings.

MORAG: Tell me more! Christie?

But CHRISTIE nods off in exhaustion and drink, snoring.

The phone keeps ringing.

***

ROYLAND: Are you going to get that?

MORAG: What?

JULES: Aren't ya gonna get that?

ROYLAND: The phone, are you…?

EVA: It could be me calling.

PIQUE: Or me, Ma.

CHRISTIE: *(Wakes with a start.) Answer the christly phone!*

MORAG: Oh!

MORAG comes back to reality.

MORAG: Pique? Is that you?

CRISPIN: Morag, dahling.

MORAG: Oh, hello, Crispin. How's New York?

ROYLAND: I'll be off. Thanks for the drink.

CRISPIN: Busier than the boondocks, I'm sure.

ROYLAND: Divining at Smith's next week.

MORAG nods. ROYLAND leaves.

CRISPIN: Morag…

MORAG: I know.

CRISPIN: The publisher is waiting. It's been five years. They've been very patient, but—

MORAG: Soon, I promise. I've started something…

CRISPIN: Started?

MORAG: Please, Crispin, this is a hard one.

CRISPIN: *(Sighs.)* Morag, we've known each other a long time. Morag, you've written four fantastic novels, but there are writers out there writing a novel a year.

MORAG: A *year*? That's not writing, it's typing.

CRISPIN: It's a new world.

MORAG: I can't write a story that isn't there to be written, Crispin.

             CHRISTIE appears on a dilapidated horse-drawn cart.

CHRISTIE: Do you want to come along, lass?

CRISPIN: The past doesn't pay the bills, Morag.

MORAG: *(Eyeing CHRISTIE.)* That's what I'm worried about.

                         ***

             She gets up on the cart.

CHRISTIE: Giddup!

             They travel. Or perhaps the world travels past them.

MORAG: Why do people call the place you work the "Nuisance Grounds"?

CHRISTIE: Well, it's like this. See all these houses here on Hill Street? Well, all the old, rotten stuff these people throw away is a nuisance to them. So, the town hires me to pick it up and drag it to the Nuisance Grounds.

He stops along the way to heave things onto the cart.

MORAG: Why not do something else?

CHRISTIE: I worked for the CPR, but the Depression ended that. Then the town offered me this. I'd dug graves in France during the war. Nothing worse than that. So, I took it.

Heave.

Some thinks, because I take off their muck for them, they think I'm muck. Well, I am muck, but so are they. Not a father's son, not a man born of woman, who is not muck in some part of his immortal soul.

That's what they don't realize. When I carry away their refuse, I'm carrying off part of them, do you see?

MORAG: I think so.

Heave.

They travel.

CHRISTIE: *(Like a preacher.) By their garbage shall ye know them!* I swear, by the ridge of tears and by the valour of my ancestors, I say unto you, Morag Gunn, *by their bloody christly garbage shall ye well know them!*

***

They arrive. The foul steam of the Nuisance Grounds.

Aye, here we are now.

MORAG: *(Her arm to her nose.)* The smell!

CHRISTIE: Dunnae be afraid, lass. It won't hurt ya. It's only the smell of life run its course.

He climbs aboard the back and starts shovelling off.

Now look. You see these bones here? They mean Simon Pearl the lawyer's got money for steak.

And here now. Doc MacLeod's wrapped up his rye bottles in brown paper to try to hide the fact that there are so many of them.

And here now, the Reverend George McKee, chucking out the family albums not a week after his grandmother went to her ancestors.

He is finished. Stands, with his shovel, surveying this cemetery of trash. Wipes his brow.

You know, Morag. People think I don't see what goes into the bins outside their back gates. But I do. I do. And once...

Once I saw a terrible thing.

MORAG: What was it, Christie?

CHRISTIE: ...A newborn baby. Wrapped in newspapers.

MORAG takes a sharp breath.

It fell out. Dead, of course. Hadn't gone its full term. It was so small, like a skinned rabbit.

MORAG: What, what'd you do with it?

CHRISTIE: Buried it.

MORAG: Where?

CHRISTIE: Here. In the Nuisance Grounds.

MORAG: *(Moved.)* Oh, Christie.

> *He spits.*

CHRISTIE: *(Bitter.)* That's what it was, wasn't it, a nuisance? The hell with their consecrated ground. The hell with the town cemetery. When I die, bury me here, I say.

> *JULES is there. He has an old guitar slung over his back.*
>
> *CHRISTIE wheels around, the shovel like a rifle, the instincts of a soldier.*

Show yourself!

JULES: Whoa, Christie. It's just me.

CHRISTIE: *(At ease.)* Oh...hello, Skinner. Find anything today?

JULES: Nah.

CHRISTIE: All right then. Come now, Morag.

MORAG: I think I'll walk back, Christie. Is that all right?

CHRISTIE: Be back before sundown. Skinner, you tell old Lazarus I says hello. Giddup! there, ya old swayback!

> *And he clops off.*

MORAG: Where you been, Skinner? Haven't seen you at school.

JULES: Off with Lazarus, setting traplines. Galloping Mountain way. What ya doin' here?

MORAG: Nothin'.

JULES:	Seein' the place where yer ol' man works, eh?
MORAG:	He's not my old man! My dad is dead.
JULES:	What's the diff?
MORAG:	Plenty, that's what!
JULES:	You think so, eh?
MORAG:	My family is named Gunn. We've been around here for longer than anybody in this whole town, see?
JULES:	*(Grinning.)* Not longer than mine.
MORAG:	Oh yeh? I'm related to Piper Gunn, so there.
JULES:	Who the hell's he?
MORAG:	He came from Scotland, and he led his people to the new world, because were living on the rocks in the Old Country because the Bitch-Duchess took their farms.
JULES:	*(Laughs.)* Where'd you get that crap from, eh?
MORAG:	It's true!
JULES:	My grandad, he built the first of our place, down in the Wachakwa River valley there, and that was one hell of a long time ago. He come back from the wars.
MORAG:	What wars?
JULES:	Out west there. Riel and Dumont and the battle with the English. Grandad was a better shot than them English soldiers. I got his name, see?
MORAG:	Skinner?
JULES:	No! Jules.

MORAG: Jew-els?

JULES: *(Correcting her.)* Jules! Skinner's just a
              nickname. Anyway, the Métis like my
              grandfather were always great fighters.
              My dad Lazarus taught me a song about it.
              Wanna hear it?

MORAG: Sure!

JULES: *(Singing, in French.) "Voulez-vouz écouter*
              chanter
              Une chanson de vérité?
              Le dixneuf de juin la bande des Bois-Brûlés
              Sont arrivés comme des braves guerriers.

              "Étant sur le point de débarquer
              Deux de nos gens se sont mis à crier:
              Deux de nos gens se sont mis à crier:
              Voilà l'Anglais qui vient nous attacquer!

              "Voulez-vouz écouter chanter
              Une chanson de vérité?
              Le dixneuf de juin la bande des Bois-Brûlés
              Sont arrivés comme des braves guerriers.
              Sont arrivés comme des braves guerriers.
              Sont arrivés comme des braves guerriers."

MORAG: That was— You do have a really nice voice.

              He's suddenly embarrassed.

JULES: Anyway, I gotta go.

MORAG: Where you going?

JULES: My dad Lazarus needs stuff for his still.
              My sister Piquette helps him. He makes his
              home brew, sells it to folks in town. Though
              they'll never admit buyin' it.

MORAG: Where's Piquette been? I haven't seen her in
              class.

JULES:	She missed a lot with the bone T.B. And then when she came back… She's not tough like you, Morag.
MORAG:	Or you.
JULES:	Or me. She acts tough, but she ain't. The kids, they call her names, throw shit at her. She's not long for this place, I figure. Lazarus wants her to stay and cook and keep house, but she's not much of a housekeeper.
MORAG:	What you going to do, Skinner? After high school, I mean.
JULES:	Join the army.
MORAG:	Really?
JULES:	Better than sticking around this dumb place. You?
MORAG:	I wanna go to university.
JULES:	And study what?
MORAG:	Writing. Books.
JULES:	Writing?! *(He laughs.)* Ya can't make a living writing!
MORAG:	Lots of people make their money writing!
JULES:	Hey, Morag, want to hear a real poem? *(Chanting.)* When apples are ripe, they should be plucked, When a girl is sixteen, she should be—
MORAG:	*Shut up! I'm not sixteen!*

He laughs harder.

Not till next month!

JULES:	*(Teasing her.)* Wanna do it, Morag? I can do it with Ina Spettigue any time I like. She never even charges me.

He starts undoing his pants.

As he's fiddling with his pants, she lunges at him.

Then kisses him — hard.

He is stunned.

ROYLAND is there with GORD.

ROYLAND:	Morag? You comin'?

She turns to ROYLAND.

MORAG:	Just let me finish this.

She types and speaks it in both worlds:

"I'm not afraid of you, Jules Tonnerre!"

JULES:	*(Laughs.)* I'll be seein' ya, Morag Gunn!

She rips out the paper, places it on the stack.

MORAG:	*(To ROYLAND.)* Ready.

***

ROYLAND has a Y-shaped piece of willow, one hand on each branch of the fork.

ROYLAND walks slowly. Up and down. Like the slow pace of a piper.

GORD:	Does it ever *not* work, Roy—?
MORAG:	Shh!
ROYLAND:	You don't have to "shh." I don't need quiet.
GORD:	See?

ROYLAND: Doesn't fail if the water's there. Or at least not so far.

MORAG: I tried divining once. Nothing happened.

ROYLAND: It's because you didn't have the gift.

MORAG: Not surprised. I mean, you're divining for water. Me, what in hell am *I* divining for?

GORD: Look!

             The tip of the willow wand is moving. The wood turns, moving downwards very slowly towards the earth. Magic.

             How about that!

             ROYLAND marks the spot by sticking the willow bough into it.

             And they'll find water there?

ROYLAND: Should be.

GORD: I just don't see how it's done.

ROYLAND: I don't know any more than you.

GORD: I'll call the drillers.

             He leaves. ROYLAND looks pale.

MORAG: You okay, Royland?

ROYLAND: Fine. It's just… Sometimes I get the feeling this time it might not work.

             A clap of thunder.

             (Suddenly.) Pique'll be back.

MORAG: …What?

ROYLAND: Before she goes away for good. She'll be back. I can feel it.

She stares at him, amazed.

MORAG: Royland… If something bad happened. Not to you, but to someone else. Would you have the right to tell someone?

ROYLAND: Well, I guess that depends on who you're telling.

MORAG: The world.

ROYLAND: I see. I guess the question then is "Why are you telling it?"

MORAG: It seems suddenly selfish, what I do.

ROYLAND: Only you can answer that, Morag.

Thunder. CHRISTIE appears. MORAG moves toward the memory.

CHRISTIE: "Loud, deep, and lang, the thunder bellow'd:"

ROYLAND: Looks like rain. Water from above and below.

***

Thunder.

CHRISTIE: "That night, a child might understand,
The Dev'l had business on his hand."

Rain.

CHRISTIE and MORAG sit on the covered porch.

CHRISTIE drinking from a bottle. MORAG is writing in her journal.

MORAG: Is that from Lazarus? What you drink?

CHRISTIE: You never mind what I drink, or where I get it. What you writing today?

MORAG: Just a story.

CHRISTIE: Maybe you'll get it published.

MORAG: It's not good enough.

CHRISTIE: Patience, lass. Don't cry before you're hurt.

CHRISTIE takes a swig.

MORAG: Tell me another story, Christie. About Piper Gunn.

CHRISTIE: Have you finished your schoolwork, then?

MORAG: Yes.

CHRISTIE: You're a terrible liar, Morag Gunn. But I'll tell you anyway. Because the tales of your ancestors are more important than anything in a christly textbook.

(Preaching.) We are what we know! Now: where was I?

MORAG: The bloody ship.

CHRISTIE: Ah! Now, the bloody ship!

Once again, the company members bring the story to life.

This time, MORAG tries feverishly to take it all down, and even repeats phrases.

CHRISTIE: There they were, all of them from the Sutherlands on board.

EVA: And that ship crossed the ocean…

LAZARUS: For weeks on end…

ACTOR:	And along the way, it gets struck with the devil's plague.
LACHLAN:	And many died.
ACTOR:	But then, the bloody ship arrives in the new land.
CHRISTIE:	Which was HERE, but not here.
MORAG:	Whaddya mean?
CHRISTIE:	The stupid captain landed the christly vessel, if you'll believe it, away up north there, at the wrong place. Can you feature it?
COMPANY:	*Hudson's Bay?!*
CHRISTIE:	Cold as all the shithouses of hell.
CAPTAIN/ LAZARUS:	Get off! Get off, all of ya!
MORAG:	What did they do?
PIPER:	Piper Gunn…
ENSEMBLE:	Piper Gunn.
EVA:	Takes up his kettle…
LACHLAN:	And his axe…
ACTOR:	And his tartan…
EVA:	With the brooch that says:
ENSEMBLE:	My Hope Is Constant in Thee!
CHRISTIE:	And he says to the captain!
PIPER:	What in the fiery hell are we doing in this terrible place?
CHRISTIE:	But again Piper's woman…

SCOTS MORAG/PIQUE

MORAG: Morag Gunn!

CHRISTIE: Aye, Morag Gunn.

SCOTS MORAG/
PIQUE: Morag steps forward...

CHRISTIE: For she had the...

ENSEMBLE: Second sight.

CHRISTIE: And she said to those assembled:

SCOTS MORAG/
PIQUE: We have arrived in this new country. And
                   here we will remain. And if we must live here,
                   in this almighty godforsaken land, with all
                   manner of beasts and frozen ice, at least let
                   us be piped onto it!

CHRISTIE: And so Piper did just that. And what did the
                   Suther-landers do?

MORAG: They rose and followed!

ENSEMBLE: They rose and followed!

SCOTS MORAG/
PIQUE: Play, Piper Gunn!

                   The company members wander off.

CHRISTIE: And a thousand miles they walked, to
                   Winnipeg.

MORAG: They couldn't have walked from Hudson's
                   Bay. It's not possible.

CHRISTIE: Well, maybe they didn't walk for all of it, but
                   a christly many miles they did.

MORAG: And then what happened?

CHRISTIE: They fought the Indians.

MORAG: Really?

CHRISTIE: They fought the half-breeds, I tell ya.

MORAG: You mean the Métis?

CHRISTIE: Whatever you call them. They fought them.
And slew them in their dozens, girl.

MORAG: Why?

CHRISTIE: Why what?

MORAG: Why did they kill them?

CHRISTIE: Why?
Because.
They were…
There.

> *A ruckus — shouting and such. The rain
> has stopped.*

GUS   *Comst hair,* you little bitch!

***

> *GUS is drunk, with a belt or stick in his
> hands. He wears standard Mennonite
> farming overalls and hat.*
>
> *EVA runs up the stoop to MORAG.*

EVA: Leafe me alone!

GUS: Come back here, *maedel*, or I'll give you twice
as worse.

MORAG: Eva! What's wrong?

GUS: None for you to care. Back inside the house,
you *hure.*

EVA:	*Nay*, I won't!

GUS moves toward them, but CHRISTIE steps into his way.

CHRISTIE: Now now, Gus Winkler.

GUS: Mind your own business, Christie Logan.

CHRISTIE: Now Gus, is there any reason to be hitting the poor girl?

GUS: Gets out of my ways!

CHRISTIE: That's enough, I said.

GUS: Look at youse. *Du schmutzig* rag picker. *Du* and *deena* little Indian-loving stray! And *du* calls yourself a *vater*?

CHRISTIE quickly and efficiently puts him into a stranglehold. He speaks quietly to him.

CHRISTIE: There'll be no more talk like that, Gus Winkler, you hear me? And no more violence towards the girl. Or I'll tell your missus all about that little wee one I found in the Nuisance Grounds. Understood?

He lets him go.

GUS: Wait till you gets home, Eva.

GUS stumbles off.

EVA: He, he wants me to do *tings*, and I…

MORAG: It's okay, Eva, you can stay here tonight. Can't she, Christie?

CHRISTIE: For as long as she needs.   You'll not be a nuisance here.

LACHLAN appears.

LACHLAN: I'll start you off at $10 a week.

CHRISTIE: Take Eva in and make her some tea.

LACHLAN: You can work full time during the summer, and part-time your last year at school.

CHRISTIE: And then keep writing your story. It may be your way out of this stinkin' town.

***

LACHLAN: That all right? Morag?

MORAG: Oh yes. Thank you, Mr. Lachlan.

LACHLAN: This is your desk, and this is your typewriter.

MORAG: My own typewriter?

LACHLAN: Were you expecting stone and chisels? Here's the weekly rundown: Obituaries. Town Council meetings. Courthouse cases, if any. Local Reports from South Wachakwa Valley. Rotary Club dinners, School Board meetings. And finally: News.

MORAG: What kind of news?

LACHLAN: Accidents, Broken Legs, Lightning Striking Barns. And updates from, from uh, the War.

>   *LACHLAN pauses — he takes a heavy breath.*

MORAG: ...Mr. Lachlan?

LACHLAN: I'm fine. Now obviously you can't be in all these places all the time. So many of these items are written down by people and sent in. And your job is to retype them. Got it?

MORAG: Got it.

LACHLAN: Here's one:

> MRS. BROWN *appears in a fancy hat.*
> *She speaks the wrong spelling and lack of*
> *punctuation.*

MRS. BROWN: Mrs. H. Brown widow of late Henry respected
                farmer spend the weekend—

MORAG: —It should be spent, not spend—

MRS. BROWN: —the weekend visiting with her son Simon
                and wif, in Manwaka and a good time had by
                all at a tea given in her hounor—

MORAG: There's no punctuation and the spelling is—

MRS. BROWN: *(Faster.)* and four kinds cak served glad you
                had a good visit Mrs. Pearl and welcon bake!

MORAG: Why can't I rewrite this?

LACHLAN: Because. They want it "as it is." You can clean
                up the spelling.

MORAG: But Mr. Lachlan, it makes the *Banner* look like
                a small-town paper.

LACHLAN: Now listen carefully, Morag. Everyone
                around these parts reads the *Manawaka*
                Banner, everyone. From the mayor to the
                farmers fifty miles from here. We *are* a small-
                town paper, Morag. And if you think you're
                too big for that, I suggest you make $10 a
                week off your *own* writing.

MORAG: Yes, Mr. Lachlan. I'm sorry, I didn't—

LACHLAN: Here.

MORAG: What's this?

LACHLAN:	A notepad.
MORAG:	What for?
LACHLAN:	What for? *You're a reporter! Go report!*

***

ROYLAND:	Picked up your mail, Morag.
PIQUE:	Dear Ma.

Letter. With a postcard inside.

MORAG:	Oh!
ROYLAND:	Who from?
MORAG:	Pique! Finally.
ROYLAND:	Where from?
PIQUE:	Made it to Thunder Bay.
PIQUETTE:	*(Laughs.)* Tonnerre Bay.
MORAG:	*(On the card.)* "The Sleeping Giant"
PIQUE:	Caught a lift with a nice-enough trucker who took me as far as Toronto, then a travelling salesman all the way to the Sault. Then a young hippie couple all the way here.
ROYLAND:	Where's she sleep?
PIQUE:	Sleeping in campgrounds when it's warm, and Trudeau hostels when it's not.
MORAG:	Oh God…
ROYLAND:	She safe?
PIQUE:	They keep calling us "Transient Youths" like it's a bad thing. Lots of us on the roads, so it feels safe.

MORAG:	She's safe.
PIQUE:	They call this hill the Sleeping Giant. Know why? The Ojibway giant Nanabijou was turned to stone when he told the secrets of the land to the white men.
PIQUETTE:	Sssecretsss.
PIQUE:	Good lesson, huh?
ROYLAND:	She sounds like her mother.
PIQUE:	I wonder if it flows the other way. Wonder if you can bring something to life by telling it the truth?
ROYLAND:	And writes like her, too.
PIQUE:	Truth, Ma. Not fiction.
ROYLAND:	I'll drop by tomorrow. With a fish.
MORAG:	Thanks.

MORAG turns to see JULES, in uniform.

***

JULES:	Is Morag home, Christie?
MORAG:	Skinner?
CHRISTIE:	She is.
MORAG:	*(Surprised.)* What are you doing here?
JULES:	On leave. Wanna go for a walk?
MORAG:	Sure, just give me a minute.

She goes off to grab a sweater.

CHRISTIE:	Fighting for King and Country.

JULES:	Cameron Highlanders. A Tonnerre in a kilt, can you imagine, Christie?
CHRISTIE:	Well, boy, stay alive, that's my advice.
JULES:	I joined for the pay. I don't aim to get hurt.
CHRISTIE:	That's the spirit.
MORAG:	Ready! Jewels!

He laughs and she hugs him.

***

The world travels by them.

JULES:	He's quite a guy, that Christie.
MORAG:	Glad *you* think so.
JULES:	Don't you?
MORAG:	Everyone laughs at him.
JULES:	Well, let 'em. Nobody else'll do that work.
MORAG:	How're things?
JULES:	Army keeps a guy busy.
MORAG:	What happens when the war ends?
JULES:	Dunno. I'd like to be a lawyer.
MORAG:	A lawyer!?
JULES:	Think I can't?
MORAG:	No, just the opposite.
JULES:	So I asked Mr. Pearl in town, how I'd do that — be a lawyer. He smiled, says:
MR. PEARL:	A person like *you*, Skinner, might do well to set their sights a bit lower.

JULES: I thought about breaking his jaw, but it'd only land me in the clink.

MR. PEARL vanishes.

MORAG: I'm sorry, Skinner.

JULES: I don't give a damn. Never have. Never will. I hate this town.

MORAG: Me, too.

JULES: Come on, I wanna show you something.

They travel.

***

JULES: This here's the Wachakwa River, though it's so shallow and narrow, it may as well be a crick.

She moves down to the water.

She is staring down into the water.

MORAG: Look at that, Skinner. The water's brown, no…amber. Amber. You can still see straight to the bottom.

JULES: Will you look at that. Amber and clear at the same time. Like a beer bottle.

MORAG: Like glass, yeh. It's beautiful.

JULES: You're beautiful.

JULES takes her now and lays her down in the grass.

MORAG takes off her glasses, slowly. And they kiss again. It's hot and frantic now. Their hands are all over each other, trying to get clothing undone. It's sexy and clumsy and fun, this youthful passion.

JULES: You remember that time at the Nuisance Grounds?

MORAG: Yeh.

JULES: And I told you about Ina Spettigue? That was a pack of lies.

                MORAG laughs. So does he.

                They kiss. MORAG pulls her hips to him and begins moving back and forth. She can't wait to get his clothes off.

JULES: *(Breathing heavy.)* Easy…easy… Not so quick.

MORAG: *(On the verge.)* Please, don't stop. Don't stop!

                And they both have an orgasm, quietly. They hold each other tightly.

                A pause.

                They look at each other.

                And both of them laugh… out of love and vulnerability.

MORAG: Oh, Skinner…

JULES: Could you call me by my real name?

MORAG: Okay. Jewels.

JULES: You say it funny. Jewels.

MORAG: How, then?

JULES: Jules.

MORAG: Jew-els.

JULES: *(Laughs.)* You better learn French, kid.

                                    ***

LAZARUS rolls a barrel in.

LAZARUS: Piquette! Come and give your old man a hand, then.

PIQUETTE: *J'arrive!*

PIQUETTE enters carrying some firewood.

LAZARUS: Did you leave that door open, *la pchite*?

PIQUETTE drops the firewood and goes out the way she came.

LAZARUS: *(Calling after her.)* You don't want them vapours gathering up.

PIQUETTE comes back.

PIQUETTE: It's open. I propped it open.

LAZARUS: One little spark and —

PIQUETTE: I know, boom.

LAZARUS: Boom.

PIQUETTE: I'll get the jugs.

PIQUETTE leaves. MORAG and JULES come in.

LAZARUS: Skinner, *regardés toi*?

JULES: Hey, Dad!

LAZARUS: *(Michif.) Ta vnu back, eh?* (You're back, eh?)

JULES: *(Michif.) Ink powr in pchi bowt ten.* (Just for a while.)

LAZARUS: *(Michif.) A bin, den no ayn min avek l'bari — y li kazimen prey a et mi dan li krush.* (Well, give us a hand with this barrel — it's about ready to be put in the jugs.)

JULES does.

LAZARUS: Who are you?

JULES: This here is Morag Gunn. You know. From over at Christie Logan's place.

LAZARUS: Oh. Yeh. I know Christie.

PIQUETTE: Jules!

     PIQUETTE runs to JULES and hugs him.

JULES: Hi, Piquette. You know Morag, from town?

MORAG: Hi, Piquette.

PIQUETTE: Morag.

LAZARUS: Want some bannock, Morag?

MORAG: Sure.

     LAZARUS gestures, PIQUETTE exits.

JULES: Ya should move it outside, Dad. Safer.

LAZARUS: Yeh, and then I got the RCMP down my neck. No *marsi*.

MORAG: How do you know Christie, Mr. Tonnerre?

LAZARUS: Worked as section hands on the CPR, but that quit in the Depression, eh. It's the same everywhere, Christ-awful jobs and treated like *la merde*. At least we can live down here in the valley. Better than living on those road allowances up near town.

     PIQUETTE enters with bannock, offers it to MORAG; MORAG eats.

LAZARUS: My *maman's* recipe, eh. Passed down from her mother, and her mother before her.

MORAG: This is good.

LAZARUS: Every recipe is a story.

MORAG takes out her journal.

MORAG: Mr. Tonnerre, I hear you tell stories, from the old days.

JULES: *(A hiss.)* Morag!

LAZARUS: He told you that, eh?

MORAG: Can you tell me one? I like stories.

LAZARUS: Well, okay. I'll tell you the story of Jules's grandfather, the one he was named after *(Michif)* *Y'a lonten, Jules Tonnerre…* (A long time ago, Jules Tonnerre…)

JULES: Dad, she doesn't understand Michif.

LAZARUS: *(French.) Jules, va-chercher ta guitare.* (Jules, get your guitar.)

Jules does.

It's better to sing a story. That way you remember it, see?

The company members gather to tell/sing this in a way that is appropriate to Métis culture.

JULES/
LAZARUS: *(Singing, in Michif.) Li Michif ki lon renkontri di tot la prayri*
Powr gardi lewr tayr, powr li gardi lib,
Y son renkontri labaw dan Qu'Appelle valley
O koti di lewr chef, Louis Riel.

JULES: *(Singing.)* They took their rifles into their hands
They fought to keep their mothers' lands,
And one of them who gathered there was

ENSEMBLE: *(Singing.)* A Métis boy called Jules Tonnerre.

JULES/
LAZARUS: *(Singing.)* He is not more than eighteen years;
He will not listen to his fears.
(Michif.) Son kewr y li vray, son kewr y li for,
He knows the land where his people belong.

GUS: *(Spoken.)* Macdonald, he sits in Ottawa
Drinking down his whiskey raw.

Sends out west ten thousand men,
Swears the Métis will not rise again.

It was near Batoche, in Saskatchewan,
The Métis bullets were nearly gone.

If I was a wolf, I'd seek my lair,
But a man must try, said Jules Tonnerre.

JULES/
LAZARUS: *(Singing.)* Jules Tonnerre and his brothers,
They fought like animals, fought like hell.
Before the earth will take our bones,

ENSEMBLE: *(Singing.)* We'll load our muskets with nails
and stones.

JULES/
LAZARUS: *(Singing.)* Riel, he was hanged in Regina one
day;
Dumont, he crossed the U.S.A.

Jules's voice is one the wind will tell
In the prairie valley that's called Qu'Appelle.

ENSEMBLE: *(Singing.)* They say the dead don't always die.
They say the truth outlives the lie—

JULES/
LAZARUS: The night wind calls their voices there.
(Michif.) L'om Michif, kom

ENSEMBLE:	*Jules Tonnerre.* *Kom Jules Tonnerre.* *Kom Jules Tonnerre.* *Kom Jules Tonnerre.* *Kom Jules Tonnerre.*
	The company vanishes.
MORAG:	They told us in school that Riel was crazy.
LAZARUS:	Those books — written by white people. He wasn't crazy. He just had second sight.
MORAG:	Second sight?
LAZARUS:	He could see inside a man's head, what they're thinking. And that scared the crap out of those white men.
MORAG:	But that wasn't the end, that battle, was it?
LAZARUS:	No, by God. No, that was just the beginning. After they murdered Riel, they stole everything from us. Our land. Our kids. They left us with nothing. *Rien!*
JULES:	Dad.
LAZARUS:	All those people in town, they all think they're better than us. Your old man, Christie, he's okay.
MORAG:	He's not— Yes. Yes, he is.
LAZARUS:	We trade stories, him and me.
JULES:	All right, Dad. That's enough for now. I got to get Morag back. I'm leaving tomorrow morning.
MORAG:	Tomorrow?
LAZARUS:	So soon?

JULES:	Army truck waiting at the bus station to pick us all up.

> *He gets up. So does MORAG. As LAZARUS speaks to JULES, PIQUETTE moves closer to MORAG.*

JULES:	Dad.
PIQUETTE:	Hey, Morag.
MORAG:	Hey, Piquette.
PIQUETTE:	I'm getting married, eh? Getting out of this jerkwater place.
JULES:	*(To LAZARUS.)* Now I'm in the army, *(Michif.) j'a in pchi brin d'arjen.* (I got a bit of money.)
MORAG:	*(To PIQUETTE.)* Married? Wow. That's— that's—
JULES:	*(To LAZARUS, in Michif.) Porkway ki ji peyl paw* (Why don't I pay for you to) get some new teeth put in?
PIQUETTE:	*(To MORAG.)* Surprised, eh?
MORAG:	N-no. Who?
PIQUETTE:	He's an English fella, works in the stockyards in the city there.
LAZARUS:	*(Michif.) Marsi, mi j'marawnj bin san uzot.* (Thanks, but I'm getting along okay without them.)
MORAG:	Well, congratulations — good luck —
PIQUETTE:	So you probably won't see me again.
MORAG:	I hope you'll be happy.

PIQUETTE hugs MORAG, hard.
LAZARUS hugs JULES.

LAZARUS: Skinner, you look out, eh? And Morag, you
say hi to old Christie. He's a good man.

MORAG: Okay.

LAZARUS retreats. PIQUETTE runs up,
and hugs JULES.

JULES: *(In French.) Prendre ça pour la marriage.* (Take
this for the wedding.)

He hands her some cash.

PIQUETTE: *(French.) Prendre soin, Jules.* (Take care, Jules.)

She looks back at MORAG, and then leaves.

MORAG: Piquette told me she's getting married.

JULES: Yeh. *(Shaking his head.)* I think she's got herself
a first-rate no good, but—

MORAG: But?

JULES: Who am I to judge her? I joined the army to
get out of here.

JULES puts his arm around her and they
walk, then stop and kiss.

JULES: So long, Morag. I'll be seein' ya.

And the moment passes again between
them, as if the past and future are one.

***

The explosions of war.

Dieppe. JULES hunkered down on the
beach with a rifle and helmet. A soldier next
to him falls. He tries to help him.

A flash of light and sound and...

Silence.

***

CHRISTIE *with* Winnipeg Tribune.

CHRISTIE: Aw, Christ in heaven.

MORAG: What is it?

CHRISTIE: Those stupid bastards sent our boys to hell.

MORAG: What?

CHRISTIE: The Highlanders.

MORAG: Let me see.

She snatches it. LACHLAN appears.

LACHLAN: I want you to reprint this list from the *Winnipeg Tribune.*

***

The buddy next to JULES slowly vanishes as:

MORAG: *(Reading.)* Oh God.

LACHLAN: I want the headline to be "Our Brave Boys at Dieppe."

MORAG: There must be a hundred names here.

LACHLAN: The families from Manawaka will call in their obituaries. Make sure you're ready to take them down word for word.

MORAG: What's this?

LACHLAN: Robert's. My son. Make sure it goes at the bottom right.

MORAG: …Mr. Lachlan?

LACHLAN: Just do your job, Morag.

                    ***

             MORAG types as:

             JULES gets up slowly.

CHRISTIE: *(Reading.)* "There are many dead who will not
             be buried in the Manawaka cemetery up on
             the hill where the tall spruces stand like dark
             angels. Not until this moment has the War
             been a reality here. But now, we will never
             forget our brave boys from Manawaka."

             She looks at him.

             That's good, lass. That's real good. What of
             Jules Tonnerre?

             JULES leaves.

MORAG: *(Hopeful.)* He's not on the list.

             CHRISTIE hugs MORAG

CHRISTIE: Let's hope, lass. Go down to Lazarus, Morag,
             and tell him what you know. And while
             you're there, ask him for my medicine. My
             hands are trembling something fierce.

                    ***

MORAG: Lazarus?

PIQUETTE: He ain't here.

MORAG: Piquette. I thought you were gone to the city.

PIQUETTE: Didn't work out.

MORAG: Oh. Your fella—

PIQUETTE: My husband? Yeh, well, turned out he didn't want a wife after all.

MORAG: I'm sorry.

PIQUETTE: Not your fault. City is hard.

MORAG: It's good you came home.

PIQUETTE: *(Snorts.)* Yeh, great. Cooking and keeping the fire going. I ain't never getting out of here.

MORAG: Christie said to tell Lazarus—

PIQUETTE: *(Hands her a bottle.)* Stuff'll kill him.

MORAG: No, I mean, yes, but — Jewels. He wasn't on the list.

> *MORAG hands her the list.*

> ***

> *The phone rings.*

> *The company members stare at her.*

> *The phone keeps ringing.*

> *Finally:*

MORAG: Yes?

OPERATOR: Collect call.

MORAG: What?

OPERATOR: Collect call.

PIQUE: Ma?

> *PIQUE is there.*

MORAG: Pique, my God, how are you? Where are you?

PIQUE: I'm in Manawaka.

MORAG: Manawaka?

PIQUE: Thought I'd go and see the old place for myself, after everything you told me.

MORAG: Pique, are you okay?

PIQUE: Well, that's the thing, eh. I'm calling from the police station here.

MORAG: What?

We see some representation of the following:

PIQUE: So I'm walking along, just outside of town, hoping for a lift. A car slows past me, a bunch of middle-aged guys, and they're drunk...

RACIST 1:   Hey!

RACIST 2:   Wanna go for a ride?

RACIST 3:   How much for an hour!

PIQUE: And I take one look and think uh-uh, and wave them past. Know what they do? They start pelting empty beer bottles at me. Outta the windows. Yelling all kinds of shit.

RACIST 3:   Bitch!

RACIST 1:   Whore!

RACIST 2:   Indian!

PIQUE: Well, the glass got me on the arm, and I guess the blood kind of scared them. They took off.

The memory ends.

MORAG: *(More to herself.)* My God, my God...

PIQUE: I walked into town. Stopped at a house, asked if I could wash up. They called the cops.

MORAG: Oh, good.

PIQUE: *(Laughs.)* No. Not good. They reported *me*. I've been let off with a warning.

MORAG: You? But—

PIQUE: All they saw was a Native girl walking through town with blood on her arm, hitch-hiking. Nice hometown ya got here, Ma.

MORAG: Pique, I want you to come home.

PIQUE: I knew I shouldn't have told you.

MORAG: Pique, come home. *Now.*

PIQUE: I gotta go, Ma.

              But she is gone. LACHLAN is there.

LACHLAN: Morag. There's been a fire.

MORAG: Where?

LACHLAN: At the Tonnerre shack.

              A distant "boom."

MORAG: Oh, God.

LACHLAN: What?

MORAG: Is anyone hurt?

LACHLAN: I don't know. Get down there. See what happened.

MORAG: *(Hesitates.)* But what if...

LACHLAN: What are you waiting for?

              You're the one who thinks the *Banner* should act like a big city newspaper. Well, here's a genuine news story. Now GO!

                            ***

The Tonnerre shack.

Smoke.

MORAG approaches the memory carefully.

MORAG: Lazarus? Lazarus.

LAZARUS appears.

He comes out of his burnt shack.

He carries PIQUETTE in his arms.

He lays her down on the ground.

LAZARUS: *(French.) C'est ma fille.*

You see her?
This is my daughter.
She's mine.
She tried so hard
But all the world could see
Was

ENSEMBLE: *(Quietly.)* Bitch.

ENSEMBLE: *(Quietly.)* Whore.

ENSEMBLE: *(Quietly.)* Indian.

LAZARUS: Came home from the city
For this

This is my daughter.
This is my daughter.

LAZARUS weeps. As does MORAG.

MORAG: ....Piquette.

End of Act One

Act Two

The company members gather.

We see PIQUE surrounded by joyful Métis dancers and fiddlers.

They vanish, and PIQUE is now back at MORAG's, with her knapsack.

PIQUETTE is there and from here on, is always in MORAG's space in the present. Always observing, and often directly participating.

MORAG sees PIQUE.

MORAG: Pique! Oh my God!

She smothers her with affection.

PIQUE: Go easy.

MORAG: Are you okay? Are you hurt?

PIQUE: I'm fine.

MORAG: How did you get here?

PIQUE: Howdya think?

PIQUE takes a load off.

MORAG: Braids. I've never seen you in braids.

PIQUE: The women in Galloping Mountain wear their hair this way and I thought—

She stops herself.

MORAG: Galloping Mountain?

PIQUE: Yeh.

MORAG: But why did you—?

PIQUE: I can't talk about that. Not yet. I need to see Dad.

MORAG: *(Surprised.)*…Oh?

PIQUE: I haven't seen him in seven years.

MORAG: I realize that.

PIQUE: I need to talk to him.

MORAG: Can you tell me why?

PIQUE: I have my reasons.

MORAG: Is there something I should—

PIQUE: *I have my reasons.*

GORD enters.

GORD: Pique!

PIQUE: Oh no.

GORD: Pique, baby!

PIQUE: *I'm not your child, Gord!*

GORD: Listen to me.

PIQUE: Ah! Why did I even come back! *Leave me alone!*

She runs off. He follows.

***

PIQUETTE hands MORAG a piece of paper.

MORAG ignores it.

LAZARUS: The river is like a memory.

MORAG: Wait!

                She takes the paper and rolls it in.

CHRISTIE: It never loses its ancient power.

MORAG: *(Sitting.)* I'm not ready!

EVA: But it never ceases to be new, either.

MORAG: Give me a second!

LACHLAN: Listen, Morag.

ENSEMBLE: Listen.

                                    ***

                Sound of a train.

CHRISTIE: Well then, this is it.

MORAG: I have to go, Christie. You understand, don't
                you?

LACHLAN: Here.

MORAG: I've got to get out of Manawaka.

                LACHLAN gives her an envelope of cash.

LACHLAN: I saved this up for Robert. To go to school. He
                won't be needing it now.

MORAG: Mr. Lachlan…

CHRISTIE: You go get yourself educated.

LACHLAN: Take it. Be a writer.

EVA: Take care, Morag. Thanks for being a friend all these years.

CHRISTIE: I want you to have something, Morag.

EVA: I'll look in on Christie for ya.

CHRISTIE: Not much of a gift for a girl, I suppose.

                   The knife.

MORAG: A knife?

CHRISTIE: Traded it with a fella. Figured it may be important someday.

MORAG: What's this — carved into it?

CHRISTIE: Dunno. Didn't ask.

MORAG: *(Her heart may explode.)* Christie….

CHRISTIE: Now you listen, Morag Gunn. Go be who you are. And never come back to this place.

EVA: 'Bye, Morag. Don't forget to write!

                   MORAG watches them go. As:

                   BROOKE enters with a book, and students gather.

MORAG: "…Then since that I may know…"

                              ***

BROOKE/
MORAG: *(Reading in front of a class.)* "As liberally, as to a Midwife, shew…

BROOKE: "Thy self: cast all, yea, this white linen hence,
                   There is no penance due to innocence.
                   To teach thee, I am naked first; why then
                   What needst thou have more covering than a man."

Miss Gunn?

MORAG: Yes?

BROOKE: What do you think of the writing of Donne?

She stands.

MORAG: What I can't understand, is how Donne can write terrific lines like "Death, be not proud" and then also write so many cruel lines.

BROOKE: "Cruel," you say?

MORAG: Well, like "For God's sake hold your tongue and let me love." That's a very cruel line. You wonder what she might have said to him in return.

BROOKE: You would not take it kindly to be told to hold your tongue, Miss Gunn?

Her classmates titter.

STUDENTS: *(A quiet whispered memory.)* Mo-rag, Mo-rag, gets her clothes from an ol' flour bag!

MORAG: *(Proud.)* No. No, I would not.

BROOKE: Well, that's good to know. That is all for today.

MORAG collects her books.

Miss Gunn.

MORAG: Yes, Professor Skelton?

BROOKE: Can I see you in my office tomorrow, 4 pm? There are a few things I'd like to discuss with you.

***

ROYLAND: So, the prodigal daughter has returned.

MORAG: What's that?

ROYLAND: Pique's come back. Just like I said.

MORAG: Yes.

ROYLAND: Seen a ghost, Morag?

MORAG: How come you always know?

ROYLAND: You don't need second sight to see you're looking grim as granite.

MORAG: I am forty-seven years old, Royland. And it seems likely at this point, I'll be spending the rest of my life alone. The last thing, the only thing I had to get really right in life was raising my kid, and I screwed that up.

ROYLAND: Well. That's a first. Maybe this will help. From the Landing.

MORAG: Thanks.

                LAZARUS is there with CHRISTIE.

                A bottle from ROYLAND. A jug from LAZARUS.

CHRISTIE: Thanks.

LAZARUS: Brewed fresh today.

CHRISTIE: All I got is a dollar.

MORAG: I'm a little short on cash right now.

LAZARUS: That's all right.

ROYLAND: That's all right. I know where you live. Cheers. And remember, Morag: I don't find the water. The water finds me.

                He leaves.

                ***

BROOKE is there, with two glasses.

BROOKE: Scotch?

MORAG: Uh. I suppose, yes?

BROOKE: I always keep a bottle in my office. For reflection.

> *He pours. She's never had Scotch. She sips. It burns.*

BROOKE: I've enjoyed having you in the class.

MORAG: It's my favourite subject. And you make it easy to enjoy.

BROOKE: I read your short story. In this week's *Veritas*.

MORAG: You did?

BROOKE: "Fields of Green and Gold." I thought it extremely promising. The ending is sentimental, but—

MORAG: It needs to be rewritten. It's not right. There's something missing.

BROOKE: I'm happy to look at it if you think I could help.

MORAG: *(Honoured.)* Thank you.

> *There is obviously an awkward attraction.*

BROOKE: Did you grow up here? In Winnipeg?

MORAG: No. I'm from up Galloping Mountain way.

BROOKE: "Galloping Mountain way"?

MORAG: A small town.

BROOKE: Your family lives there?

MORAG: My parents died when I was very young. I was brought up by…an acquaintance.

BROOKE: That sounds like it was a lonely sort of life.

MORAG: No more than most.

BROOKE: There is an aura of mystery surrounding you, Morag Gunn. Which I find very, very….

> *He goes in for a kiss. She stops him. Removes her glasses.*

> *She's ready now.*

> *He kisses her. She responds — willingly.*

I like you, Morag.

MORAG: Professor Skelton—

BROOKE: Brooke. Out of class.

MORAG: I like you too, Brooke.

BROOKE: I am so much older than you.

MORAG: It doesn't bother me.

BROOKE: You seem very sure.

MORAG: I'm always sure. With things that matter.

> *ROYLAND is there.*

> *He slaps the fish on the table:*

***

ROYLAND: Morag!

MORAG: Ah!

ROYLAND: This here's for Pique's breakfast.

MORAG: *(Recovering.)* Right.

ROYLAND: I'm divining today. Think Pique'd like to come?

MORAG: She'd love that. But she's still asleep.

ROYLAND: I'll wait.

MORAG: She's eighteen: you could be waiting a long time.

> *ROYLAND laughs.*
>
> *PIQUETTE is there, rummaging through some boxes.*

Royland. The divining. How did you start?

ROYLAND: Well. Long time ago... I was a preacher.

MORAG: WHAT?

ROYLAND: Yup. One of your real ripsnortin' Bible-punchers. I was married then, too.

MORAG: The surprises keep coming!

ROYLAND: Still keep a picture of her.

> *He wipes his hands. He pulls out a photo. Hands it to MORAG.*

We married young, just before The Call came upon me. For all them years I was dead set against drink, tobacco, dances, cards, lace curtains, any dress that looked like anything but a gunny sack. And so, my poor wife, she...

> *PIQUETTE has found a photo album.*

She led a life that was absent of anything beautiful at all. I even quit making love to her.

MORAG: What happened?

ROYLAND: She ran away. Months went by. Finally, I tracked her down. She was living in a terrible, dirty little room. Alone. Working as a waitress in a café. She looked like a ghost. I saw, soon as I laid eyes on her, what I'd done. I begged her to come back home, that I'd quit being a Bible-puncher.

MORAG: And?

ROYLAND: Next time I set eyes on her she was in the morgue.

MORAG: Oh no.

ROYLAND: Drowned herself. Didn't leave a note. Guess she had nothing left to say.

MORAG: I'm so sorry, Royland.

ROYLAND: After that I came here, to work for my aunt and uncle on their farm. And my auntie, she had the gift. And I found out, through her, that I had it too. And so, I settled here. Because it seemed better to find water than…

MORAG: Raise fire?

ROYLAND: That's good. You should be a writer.

PIQUE rushes in, and hugs ROYLAND.

PIQUE: Royland! My Old Man of the River!

ROYLAND: Good to have you home, Pique. Here's a pickerel for your breakfast.

PIQUE: Thanks! My favourite! You know something? You made a big mistake in not having children. You'd make a fine granddad!

MORAG is mortified. ROYLAND takes the hit, but then quickly says:

ROYLAND:	Well, Pique, I always thought I was kind of like that to you.
PIQUE:	You are. You *are*!
ROYLAND:	Wanna come watch me divine a well?
PIQUE:	*Sure!* Give me a minute.

> *She leaves. MORAG hands back the picture of ROYLAND's wife.*

MORAG:	What was her name, Royland? Your wife.
ROYLAND:	Ophelia. You know what that name means?
MORAG:	*(Surprised.)* I don't, actually.
ROYLAND:	It means: "Help."
PIQUE:	Ready!
ROYLAND:	Okay!
PIQUE:	What's this?

> *The picture PIQUETTE has found.*

MORAG:	*(Surprised.)* What?
PIQUE:	Whoa, who's this handsome guy?

> *BROOKE is there. MORAG snatches the picture.*

MORAG:	Nothing. Old pictures.
BROOKE:	I have a surprise.
PIQUE:	...Okay.
ROYLAND:	Come on, Pique. Let's go find some water.

> *She and ROYLAND leave.*

***

MORAG: A surprise? What is it?

BROOKE: An offer. A tenured position. In Toronto.

MORAG: Oh, my goodness!

BROOKE: Will you come?

MORAG: Yes! Yes! Will we get married, Brooke?

BROOKE: *(Laughs.)* Normally, I would be the one making the proposal! But since you've asked, why not?

            They embrace.

MORAG: And will I go to university there, too?

BROOKE: If you want to. But on my new salary at York, I can afford to keep a wife. Why don't you simply read? Education isn't getting a degree, you know. It's learning to think.

MORAG: I'd have time to work at my own writing.

BROOKE: And care for the house, naturally.

MORAG: Of course! Oh, Brooke!

            She throws her arms around him.

BROOKE: One more thing, love. What about seeing a doctor? A diaphragm would be more reliable. We don't want any.... accidents?

MORAG: But I want a child of yours, Brooke. Someday.

            MORAG is grabbing at BROOKE — trying to get his clothes off. He resists.

            PIQUE bursts in — GORD behind her.

PIQUE: Gord!

GORD: Listen, I got a plan. A real plan! Hi, Morag.

BROOKE: Lots of time for that, little one. Lots of time.

                                    ***

PIQUE: Are we disturbing your writing?

MORAG: *(Yes.)* Well…

PIQUE: So what's this plan?

GORD: *(A headline.)* Horses!

PIQUE: Horses.

GORD: I was raised on a ranch. We bred palominos in Alberta. They're worth a lot. We'll put out the land as feed crops. Royland says he'll put up some bread for a coupla nags and I've got a few hundred bucks put by as well.

PIQUE: And then what?

GORD: I'll give riding lessons!

            MORAG and PIQUE exchange doubtful looks.

            What! I can teach Western *and* English. And as soon as we've got all this bloodstock, we'll sell one or two to make more money.

MORAG: And who's going to *take* these riding lessons?

PIQUE: Stay out of this, Ma. *(To GORD.)* And who's going to *take* these riding lessons?

GORD: People! From town. And parts. Nearby.

PIQUE: And where am I in this whole deal?

GORD: One of us needs to get a job in McConnell's Landing. Until this thing takes off.

PIQUE: And that would be me.

GORD: Just until—

PIQUE: No.

GORD: Pique!

PIQUE: I don't want to be here anymore.

GORD: You just came back.

PIQUE: I need to leave. For good.

GORD: Where then?

PIQUE: West.

MORAG: West?

GORD: Noooo.

PIQUE: Why?

GORD: Cuz that's where *I* grew up.

PIQUE: Then you see my point.

He's basically on his knees without the ring.

GORD: Please, Pique. You're part of who I am.

PIQUE: Gord, look. I really care about you, I do, but …Ma, help me out!

MORAG: Pick some strawberries?

PIQUE takes off. GORD looks at MORAG.

GORD: I get this feeling you don't like me that much, Morag.

MORAG: And why would you say that?

GORD: You hardly ever call me by my name.

MORAG: That's it? When did young people get so easily offended?

GORD:	We're a different generation. We have our *own* things we get offended by.
MORAG:	How can I help you? *Gordon.*
GORD:	Why would Pique want to take off again?
MORAG:	That's not a question for me to answer.
GORD:	I can't go back there. I hated Alberta when I lit out.
MORAG:	I felt exactly the same about the town where I grew up. But then…
GORD:	What?
MORAG:	The whole town is still alive, inside my head. And won't leave me alone.
GORD:	That's terrible.
MORAG:	It's actually not.
GORD:	I don't know who I am! But I know whatever it is, it's gotta be with Pique.
MORAG:	People aren't horses, Gord. You can't saddle someone with your own dreams, just because you think they're important to have on the ride.
GORD:	I'm so *confused*!
	He leaves.
BROOKE:	*Mrs.* Morag *Skelton*!

***

MORAG is writing to CHRISTIE. BROOKE helping her.

MORAG:	Dear Christie:

LAZARUS: Christie Logan.

CHRISTIE: Lazarus Tonnerre.

MORAG: I'm getting married!

LAZARUS: Here.

A jug.

CHRISTIE: Thanks.

LAZARUS: Brewed fresh today.

MORAG: His name is Brooke Skelton, and he teaches here at the university.

BROOKE: I'm an Englishman!

MORAG: He is an Englishman.

CHRISTIE: Swig?

LAZARUS: Sure.

MORAG: As I am not yet twenty-one, I need your permission. You will say okay, though, right?

LAZARUS: Got anything for me this week, Christie?

CHRISTIE: Nothing worth trading.

MORAG: We are getting married at City Hall, so we're not having any guests. I hope you don't mind. We will be moving to Toronto soon afterwards.

CHRISTIE: I'm a little short on cash right now.

LAZARUS: *(Friendly.)* It's okay, Christie. I know where you live.

LAZARUS vanishes. CHRISTIE takes a swig.

CHRISTIE: Well, you are getting married, that is some news all right, and you know damn well I would not say no, and it is your life, and I hope all goes well. Too bad he is English and not Scots, ha ha. P.S. A little something for the honeymoon.

He gives MORAG a one-dollar bill.

She is ashamed.

***

STYLIST 1:   Now, Mrs. Skelton, you're going to *love* Toronto. But we're going to have to do something with your hair. *(Overlapping with speech below.)* Shorter, a few curls, a little swirl over the brow…

STYLIST 2:   …I suggest a lightly tailored suit for the daytime, and maybe some frills. *(Overlapping with speech below.)* And of course you'll need a black cocktail dress for Professor Skelton's events….

STYLIST 3:   …It's all about the eyes, Mrs. Skelton: Trace your crease with a black eyeliner if you want to make more of a statement.

BROOKE: You look fabulous, love. Like a real professor's wife. Now, what have you made us for dinner?

***

PIQUETTE reads over MORAG's shoulder.

PIQUETTE: *(Blech.)* "Like a real professor's wife"?

MORAG: What's wrong with it?

PIQUETTE: Boring.

MORAG: What do you want from me?

PIQUETTE: Get on with it, Morag.

> *MORAG goes to BROOKE. She runs her hands through his hair.*

MORAG: Brooke?

BROOKE: Yes, love?

MORAG: I really think we should try to have a child, Brooke.

BROOKE: You'll be awfully tied down. You're still very young.

MORAG: But you're not.

BROOKE   *(Laughs.)* Ha! Is that right?

MORAG: I didn't mean…I'm just cooped up in here all day, I'm going crazy.

BROOKE: *(Testy.)* I never realized it was such an *ordeal* to be kept.

MORAG: *(Frustrated.)* That's not what I meant!

BROOKE: What about your writing?

MORAG: It needs to be rewritten. It's not right. There's something missing.

BROOKE: Let me be the judge. Show me.

MORAG: All right. *(Some pages.)* I've been working on a novel. It's about a woman—

BROOKE: *(Aghast; laughs.)* A NOVEL?

MORAG: Yes. A NOVEL.

BROOKE: Ha, ha. My goodness. Do you know how much *time* and *skill* it takes to write a novel?

MORAG: I'll find out, won't I?

BROOKE: I mean, a short story perhaps, for the local newspaper. But a *novel*.

MORAG: You know a lot, Brooke. But I know something, too. And it's different from just reading or teaching.

BROOKE: Well, perhaps you'd like to take over my English 450 course on the Contemporary Novel? I'm sure it could be arranged.

                    She stuffs the pages away.

MORAG: Fine. Don't look at it.

BROOKE: Now, now, *child*.

MORAG: Stop!

BROOKE: I beg your pardon?

MORAG: I'm not your child. I am your wife.

BROOKE: But you are behaving like a spoiled brat. I give you time, I give you a home, I give you—
               (Status.) What more do you want?

MORAG: All I want is everything. Now I am writing a novel. And I need to work on it tonight. So tidy up the dishes.

                    BROOKE leaves.

PIQUETTE: Here we go.

                    PIQUETTE hands MORAG paper. MORAG snatches it from her, slightly annoyed.

MORAG: I get it, I get it.

> *The explosive sound of typing – like shots being fired, one after the other.*
>
> *It grows, word by word, until she is typing furiously. As she does:*
>
> ***

LAZARUS: Here.

> *He hands a jug to CHRISTIE.*
>
> *They sit — drink.*

CHRISTIE: This town — it's good for nothing.

LAZARUS: They don't like the likes of us. Especially my kind.

CHRISTIE: And both of us veterans.

> *BROOKE is there.*

BROOKE: Hello.

CHRISTIE: Ya know, once I saw a terrible thing. Worse than the war.

BROOKE: I said HELLO.

LAZARUS: What was that?

MORAG: *(Still typing.)* Dinner isn't ready.

CHRISTIE: A newborn baby. Wrapped in newspapers.

BROOKE: What's to be done, then?

LAZARUS: And what did you do with it, Christie?

BROOKE: MORAG!

> *She stops, annoyed.*

MORAG: WHAT?

BROOKE: For God's sake, are you ill?

MORAG: I've just reached a crucial point, I can't stop
            right now.

BROOKE: *(Laughs; relieved.)* Is that all? I thought you'd
            been stricken with something serious.

MORAG: This is serious. I am writing about a stillborn
            child and the fetus has been discovered—

BROOKE: My God! Fetus? Stillborn child? What do you
            know about that? And who do you think is
            going to want to read that kind of filth?

MORAG: Go out for dinner. I need to work. GO!

***

PIQUETTE smiles at MORAG.

*And this time MORAG puts her hand out
for the paper.*

PIQUETTE hands it to her.

The company enters.

MORAG writes.

*It is an expansive, exhilarating dance,
growing and growing until...*
*... the pages are flying in the air and settling
back down on her desk.*

The novel is complete.

***

MORAG: I'm finished.

BROOKE: Finished what?

MORAG: The novel.

BROOKE: Ah! Well, let's have a look then.

MORAG: I've sent it to a publisher.

BROOKE: I see. My opinions are no longer welcomed.

MORAG: Brooke, we've been married five years.

BROOKE: *(Snide.)* Only five?

MORAG: I want a baby, Brooke.

BROOKE: Not *that* again?

MORAG: *(Angry now.)* Yes, *that* again.

BROOKE: No. Now, do I need to remind you we've been invited to the Chancellor's home tomorrow evening?

MORAG   *(Mocking.)* Not *them* again?

BROOKE: Get your hair done. You look like a witch.

MORAG: *(Mocking.)* No.

BROOKE: For God's sake!

MORAG: I won't go to those places anymore, Brooke. All those mauve-smocked little perfumed dollies floating around, making me feel fantastically inadequate.

BROOKE: Little one, you need to realize—

MORAG: *(Fierce.)* Don't!

BROOKE: What have I—?

MORAG: I am not your little one!

MORAG: I am a grown woman and have felt like I've
            been one since I was a bloody, christly kid,
            when I should have been allowed to be a
            child, but I could not, because my parents
            died!

            But now, by all the sodden saints in Beulah
            Land, at my age, I won't be called little
            one, or child, or any silly names and that's
            the everlasting christly truth of it! Do you
            understand me?

            BROOKE is in shock.

BROOKE: Are you hysterical?

MORAG: Ha!

BROOKE: Are you menstruating?

MORAG: Ha ha!

BROOKE: Are you forgetting who you are? And the
            backwater place you came from?

MORAG: Oh I'm just *beginning* to remember who I am,
            Brooke. Listen to me because I won't say this
            again.

            I won't stand to not be taken seriously. Not
            for another minute. Not by you, not by your
            snot-nosed academic friends, not by anyone.
            I won't be treated like a child. Especially if I'm
            not allowed to have one.

                        ***

            Phone rings.

CRISPIN: Mrs. Skelton?

CHRISTIE: The courage of a falcon…

MORAG: Yes?

CRISPIN: My name's Milward Crispin.

CHRISTIE: ...and the beauty of a deer...

MORAG: Yes?

CRISPIN: Walton and Pierce have accepted your manuscript for *Spear of Innocence*.

CHRISTIE: ...and the faith of saints.

MORAG: Wha-what?

CRISPIN: They thought you'd want representation.

MORAG: I don't understand.

CRISPIN: You need an *agent*, Mrs. Skelton. Do you understand?

MORAG: I see, yes.

CRISPIN: I will see to the contract, and they will assign you an editor. I'm thinking of a three thousand advance.

MORAG: Three thousand...dollars?

CRISPIN: Of course, there will be royalties after that if it sells. That's not bad for a first-time author, Mrs. Skelton.

MORAG: Ms. Crispin, there's one thing I want to make clear.

CRISPIN: And that is?

CHRISTIE: My Hope is Constant in Thee.

MORAG: My name — the name on the book? It should be Morag *Gunn*.

CRISPIN: I see. Done.

***

REVIEWER 1:   A first novel of some wit and perception.

REVIEWER 2:   A spicy and exciting novel about abortion.

REVIEWER 3:   *Spear* is a winner.

> *Looking at the dust jacket.*

BROOKE: By Morag GUNN. Well, well.

JULES: Morag Gunn!

> ***

> *JULES, a guitar case in hand.*

JULES: How about that, eh? Never thought I'd run into you again!

MORAG: Jewels!

JULES: Ha! You still say "Jewels."

MORAG: What are you doing in Toronto?

JULES: After the war, I went back to Manawaka, but I had to get outta that town. Been here five years!

MORAG: Doing what?

JULES: Guess! *(Holds up the guitar.)*

MORAG: *(Delighted.)* No!

JULES: Singing and playing in bars!

MORAG: That's great!

JULES: None of it pays good. But it's better than working in a lousy factory. Heard you married a *pro-fessor*.

MORAG: Actually, I'm writing. Published.

> *She pulls out a copy.*

JULES: Wow! You did it! Made money writing! *(Honest.)* Good for you, Morag.

MORAG: Jewels. Come back to my place for dinner, will you?

JULES: Sure?

MORAG: I'm always sure. With things that matter.

                                    ***

                        She pours them Scotches.

JULES: You should see me. Satin shirt with a lotta beadwork, and sometimes a phony doe-skin jacket with fringes and a lotta plastic porcupine quills.

MORAG: That's…bad, isn't it?

JULES: It's a load of shit, but they let me sing. Got kids, Morag?

MORAG: *(Resentful.)* No. You?

JULES: Not as far as I know. Ha. I can't stay in one place for long.

MORAG: How's Lazarus?

JULES: Oh. He, he died, eh.

MORAG: What?

                        During the following:

                        LAZARUS is there.

                        The fiddler returns and plays a lament.

JULES: Doc said it was pneumonia. Somebody found him. Called the town. I wanted to bury him in the valley, beside the shack, but not allowed.

OFFICIAL: You can't just bury bodies anywhere, Skinner.

JULES: The town graveyard then.

OFFICIAL: Not allowed.

JULES: Why not?

OFFICIAL: The Protestants won't have him in their section and the Catholics won't neither, as he died without a priest.

JULES: Didn't want his Métis bones spoiling their cemetery.

MORAG: That's terrible.

LAZARUS: Take me north, son.

JULES: So I took him Galloping Mountain way. Back of a truck. Métis churchyard there.

LAZARUS: This is good, Skinner. This is good, my boy.

JULES: No headstones. Just wooden crosses, plain pine.

LAZARUS: I like it up here.

JULES: And that was that.

She puts her hand gently on his.

MORAG: I'm glad to see you, Skinner.

JULES: I sense you're not very happy, Morag?

MORAG: Not very, no.

JULES: Care to say why?

BROOKE enters.

BROOKE: Morag?

MORAG:	Brooke, this is Jules Tonnerre. An old friend from Manawaka. He's going to stay for dinner.
JULES:	Hey.

Tension.

BROOKE:	Morag, may I speak with you?
MORAG:	*(To JULES.)* Just a second.

Within JULES's earshot:

BROOKE pours a stiff one and downs it. He sizes up the bottle.

BROOKE:	My my, your past certainly is catching up with you.
MORAG:	*(Steaming.)* I met him, on the street, by accident.
BROOKE:	Charles and Donna Pettigrew are coming over this evening.
MORAG:	What does that matter?
BROOKE:	It may not matter to you, but it does to me. And your friend seems to have gone through a fair proportion of my Scotch.
MORAG:	*Your* Scotch?
BROOKE:	Isn't it illegal to give liquor to Indians?

JULES has his jacket on. He calls:

JULES:	I'll show myself out, Morag.
MORAG:	Wait!

She grabs her coat and goes after him.

BROOKE: Morag!

                          ***

                On the street.

MORAG: Jewels, please, stop.

                He does.

                What he said was terrible.

JULES: It goes in one ear and out the other with me.

MORAG: I can't go back there. Ever.

                She may vomit.

JULES: Can you walk?

MORAG: Yes.

JULES: I know you can walk on the outside, can you walk — on the inside?

                She nods yes.

                Come on, then.

                          ***

                At his apartment.

JULES: It's not much. But it's home.

MORAG: Jewels, I'm sorry. This isn't your trouble. You've got your own.

JULES: You want to talk, or what?

MORAG: I guess sometimes you see things suddenly and then you know you've known them a long time. I gotta... *(She starts to get up.)*

JULES: Hey, you only just got here.

MORAG: I should be getting…

JULES: "Should," for God's sake, forget it. You don't want to go.

MORAG: I looked for your name, after Dieppe. I checked the casualty lists, always.

JULES: Yeh. Well. It wasn't quite the way the papers told it. All any guy thinks of is staying alive.

MORAG: How long, how long did it—?

JULES: A million years. Coupla hours. Who knows. You go kind of crazy, like. You just think, well, that's Robert Lachlan dead.

MORAG: Robert Lachlan?

JULES: Right next to me when he got it.

            He was shot in the guts. Kept trying to hold them in — they were spilling out, there, ya know…

MORAG: Jewels, please stop.

JULES: You asked. People want to hear, but they don't really want to know.

            She reaches to kiss him, but he stops.

            Now. There's something you gotta tell me.

MORAG: What?

JULES: Tell me how my sister died.

MORAG: I don't want to. I can't.

JULES: I have to know.

MORAG: Lachlan sent me down there. He didn't know what it would be like.

JULES:	Go on.
MORAG:	Piquette had been home alone. The stove. It must've been a wreck of a stove.
JULES:	It was. Lazarus was always careful with it, especially when he got drunk.
MORAG:	They said Piquette was on the homebrew...
JULES:	Yeh, well, she had a lot to forget about. That man, her *husband*, picked her up when it suited him and threw her away when it suited him. Where was Lazarus?
MORAG:	He went inside. He carried her out in his arms. The air smelled of smoke and burned wood and— and— it smelled, like — I'll never...
JULES:	What?
MORAG:	I'll never forgive myself for...
JULES:	For what? FOR WHAT?

He speaks with outrage and anger at the world.

JULES:	I hate you, I hate you all.
MORAG:	Please, Jewels!
JULES:	Why did I ever....?

He pushes her away. She begins to leave.

No. Wait awhile.

She comes back to him, touches him. Then, he touches her. He smells her hair.

They make love.

It is slow and gentle — like a dance. Pain. Loss.

This joining is being done as some answer to the past. They are making something — together.

When it is done, they lie in each other's arms, their bodies intertwined.

MORAG: Skinner?

JULES: Yeh?

MORAG: I'm gonna have to go, eh.

JULES: I know. *(A real question.)* Whatcha gonna do?

MORAG: I got some money. From the novel. Enough to get out of here and get started somewhere else.

                            ***

REAL ESTATE: For Sale — Near McConnell's Landing —

MORAG: I'll write to you.

REAL ESTATE: One hour north of Toronto.

JULES: I'm not much of a letter writer.

REAL ESTATE: Eighty-acre farm, river frontage, good well.

ROYLAND: Hello.

MORAG: Hello.

ROYLAND: I'm Royland. Welcome to the community. I brought you a perch, fresh from the river.

MORAG: Thanks. And what do you do around these parts, Royland?

ROYLAND: Me? Well…I'm a diviner.

The phone rings. MORAG stares at ROYLAND.

ROYLAND   Are you going to get that?

MORAG: What?

EVA: It's me calling.

JULES: No, it's me.

CRISPIN: It's me, Morag.

***

MORAG: Hi, Crispin.

CRISPIN: Listen, Morag.

MORAG: I know, I'm broke and I don't have a book.

CRISPIN: The publisher called. If you can't get them something by the end of the month... they're cancelling the contract.

MORAG: What?

CRISPIN: It's time, Morag.

LAZARUS: *(French.) S'il temps.*

CHRISTIE: It's time.

PIQUETTE: You've got to dig deep now.

CRISPIN vanishes.

The NURSE and DOCTOR appear.

***

NURSE: Breathe, Mrs. Gunn.

MORAG: I'm not... a *Mrs.!*

NURSE: I wouldn't advertise the fact. You're lucky they're letting you have the baby here.

MORAG: *(Within the pain.)* Where should I have it? A field?

DOCTOR: Don't bear down so hard. It's coming too quickly!

MORAG: You try holding back. I can't.... I can't.

              Birth and all the beautiful noise that goes along with it.

              PIQUE is there.

              Is it all right?

DOCTOR: Certainly, she's all right.

PIQUETTE: *(Of PIQUE.)* She's beautiful.

MORAG: She? Let me see her.

NURSE: In a moment.

MORAG: Now!

DOCTOR: *(To NURSE; irritated.)* These conscious births...!

NURSE: And did you see that child? Got involved with who knows what kind of man.

PIQUETTE: A Métis man.

NURSE: And not even married!

              They vanish.

              ***

MORAG: *(To baby.)* Hello...

JULES: *(With photo.)* Dear Morag:

CHRISTIE: *(To baby.)* Dear lass.

MORAG: Hello…

JULES: You sure are crazy, Morag! But it's your choice. I hope I'll see her one of these days.

CHRISTIE: I'd love to meet the wee one, someday.

MORAG: Hello… Piquette Tonnerre Gunn.

PIQUETTE: Piquette.

MORAG: Pique. For short.

LAZARUS: *(Michif.) La pchite.*

PIQUETTE: For short.

MORAG: Pique.

***

PIQUE: Yeh?

MORAG: What do you plan to do, honey?

PIQUE: What do you mean?

MORAG: You know.

PIQUE: Oh, you mean with Gord? I told him it was over.

MORAG: Uh-oh.

PIQUE: He took it pretty well.

MORAG: Really?

PIQUE: All things considered.

MORAG: No, I mean, what do you plan to *do*?

PIQUE: *(Pissed.)* Oh, you mean, with my life.

MORAG: Can I not ask?

PIQUE: Do I have to "do" anything? Why can't I just live my life without every moment having to be a step toward some "goal" in the future?

MORAG: That's not what I meant.

PIQUE: Don't worry. I won't stay long.

MORAG: Pique.

PIQUE: When are you going to talk about it?

MORAG: Talk about what?

PIQUE: You know exactly what I mean.

MORAG: *(Testy.)* Please enlighten me.

PIQUE: There are things you haven't told me. Things I deserve to know.

MORAG: Maybe you should ask your father.

PIQUE: Oh, I have. He's coming here.

MORAG: What?

PIQUE: Day after tomorrow.

             MORAG is panicked.

MORAG: I can't, I can't have him here. Not when I'm writing—

PIQUE: Well, he's coming. Maybe then we'll all learn something. 'Cause I'm done with this game.

             PIQUE leaves as ROYLAND comes in.

ROYLAND: Well, now.

PIQUE: Hey, Royland.

ROYLAND: Where you off to?

PIQUE: Fishing. Maybe today they'll *bite*.

ROYLAND: Here. My lucky lure.

PIQUE: Thanks.

> *She's gone.*

MORAG: She hates me.

ROYLAND: She has mixed feelings. Didn't you have mixed feelings growing up?

> *MORAG sighs.*

ROYLAND: Doing a well at Tim Mackie's place next week. Interested?

> *YOUNG PIQUE comes to MORAG. Sits in her lap.*

MORAG: I don't think so. I've got my own well to find.

**

YOUNG PIQUE: Tell another story, Mama.

MORAG: Once upon a time there was a man named Piper Gunn.

CHRISTIE: He was a great tall man.

MORAG: With a voice like the drums...

CHRISTIE: And the heart of a child...

MORAG: And the strength of conviction! And he had a little girl named Pique.

YOUNG PIQUE: *(Delighted,)* He did not!

MORAG: He did!

***

YOUNG PIQUE: Tell me another story, Mama.

MORAG: Once there was a man named Jewels Tonnerre.

LAZARUS: His heart was true…

MORAG: His heart was strong…

LAZARUS: And he knew the land...

MORAG: Where his people belonged.
                  And he had a great-granddaughter named Pique.

YOUNG PIQUE: *(Delighted.)* He did not!

MORAG: He did!

***

YOUNG PIQUE: Tell me another story, Mama.

MORAG: Once your father played his guitar, and people all over the world stopped to listen.

JULES: I like that story.

MORAG: Jewels!

JULES: *(Laughs.)* Jules, for cryin' out loud! Get it right!

                  They hug. He has a guitar case.

MORAG: How'd you find me?

JULES: Your publishers gave me your address. Hell, everybody in McConnell's Landing knows you, Morag. They think you're crazy as a bedbug. Back to the small town, eh?

MORAG: Not Manawaka.

JULES: No. This her?

MORAG: Pique. Yes.

YOUNG PIQUE: Hello.

JULES: Hello. My name's…

YOUNG PIQUE: I know who you are.

JULES: Sure you do.

YOUNG PIQUE: Mama says you sing songs and people from all over the world listen.

JULES: I do.

YOUNG PIQUE: Can you play something?

JULES: Sure.

> *He takes out his guitar.*

Now, this song is a lullaby. A long time ago, your grandma would sing this to her little girls.

(Singing, in Michif.) "Faiye dedo peanutte
Maman t'aller au nasse
pour acheter une tite katin
grosse comme la tayte a tomp ti chien."

Now you hum it with me.

> *JULES and YOUNG PIQUE hum the song.*

YOUNG PIQUE: What does it mean?

JULES: It means *you* little girl, are a *peanut*. And you need to go to sleep.

> *YOUNG PIQUE laughs.*

YOUNG PIQUE: A peanut!

Ma, can you take our picture?

MORAG: Of course, honey.

A picture is taken.

It comes out of the Polaroid.

PIQUE takes it. She waves it to make it develop.

She stares at it.

She runs off.

MORAG: How long will you stay?

JULES: Just till the morning. I got a gig in Toronto tomorrow. That okay?

MORAG: Sure.

JULES: Wanna go to bed?

She smiles. He takes her glasses off.

These damn glasses of yours.

***

PIQUE hands the photo to MORAG. PIQUETTE looks at it.

PIQUE: Look at us.

MORAG: Where did you get this?

PIQUE: I've had it all along. Always kept it.

MORAG: Long time ago.

PIQUE: Not so long. When Dad comes tomorrow, I'm gonna go with him.

MORAG: Oh?

PIQUE: Yeh. We're going west.

MORAG:	…All right.
PIQUE:	You got nothing to say to that.
MORAG:	You're a grown woman now, you can do what you want.
PIQUE:	*(Frustrated.)* Ah come on!
MORAG:	What do you expect me to say?
PIQUE:	Why couldn't you have just married Dad? Why did you name me after Auntie Piquette? Why do I have to pry the answers outta you like you were a fish trying to fight its way off a lure?
MORAG:	That's good, fish on a lure, that's—
PIQUE:	Enough.
PIQUETTE:	Enough, Morag.
PIQUE:	It's time.
PIQUETTE:	It's time.
PIQUE:	It's time I heard it from your lips.
MORAG:	*(Angry.)* You know, I have done everything, everything in my power to give you the best upbringing a kid could have.
PIQUE:	With no father around?
MORAG:	Maybe I should've brought you up in the city, where you'd have known how bad things can be. But no, I gave you an island, this perfect place in the country, so you wouldn't have to face…
PIQUE:	Face what? *(Poking,)* Use your *words*, Ma.

MORAG:	My God, the ingratitude!
PIQUE:	(*Incredulous.*) Really? *You* ever been called a dirty half-breed? *You* ever had someone throw beer bottles at you from a car? I should be grateful for that?
MORAG:	I always tried to protect you.
PIQUE:	Yeh, from who I *am*! I was brought up by *you*. I never got the other side.
MORAG:	I told you what I could.
PIQUE:	Oh, sure. Piper Gunn and Jules Tonnerre. *Stories. Words.* Why didn't you take me to see Christie? Or Lazarus? They were mine too.
MORAG:	You don't know what it was like.
PIQUE:	Because you never told me the truth. You're ashamed. You're ashamed of Dad and his family, and you're ashamed of me.
MORAG:	I *was* ashamed. I was. But not of Jules, not of you.
PIQUE:	Then of what?

MORAG is frozen.

The sound of a growing fire in her mind.

PIQUETTE:	She deserves to know.
PIQUE:	Ashamed of WHAT?
PIQUETTE:	She carries my name.

MORAG takes a big breath.

MORAG:	*I was ashamed of me. About where I came from.* About what happened. To Piquette.

PIQUE: I know what happened. She was brewing booze for Lazarus. Booze he sold to half the town, including Christie Logan, because that's the only way he could support his family. She left the door to the still closed and no one came to help. I know all that, Ma.

MORAG: No. You don't. Because I was there.

PIQUE: What?

MORAG: I was sent down. By the paper. A cold day in winter. I saw it. The shacks, all of them, burned to the ground. The smoke curling up into the sky. The air smelling of burning wood and...

She'd been ...burned alive. And Lazarus, he came out with her in his arms and....

Piquette wanted more, more than she could ever get, could ever be, in that jerkwater place, and she tried, she tried to get out, but the world just wouldn't let her, it drove her back to that shack, that life. I had seen her around town. After she got back from the city. I could have talked to her. Helped her somehow. And what did I do?

I turned my back. I turned my back on everything. On the town, on Christie. I turned my back on it all. Because I could.

That's why I'm ashamed. And I've spent my whole life trying to write that shame away.

PIQUE: So you had me out of guilt.

MORAG: No! I had you out of love! I named you out of love, too. To bind us together, your dad, his dad, and me.

PIQUE: You did that for you. You wrote all those people out of my life, *for you*. So how am I supposed to really know who I am, Ma?

She leaves. PIQUETTE follows her.

***

EVA: Morag? It's Eva. You need to come back now.

***

MORAG: Thanks for everything.

EVA: It was the least I could do. He was so good to me when I was young. He saved me, ya know. And I couldn't have children. So it was nice to care for someone.

MORAG: Where is he?

EVA: Through there. Morag... The stroke. He can't... Christie can't talk.

MORAG approaches CHRISTIE, asleep.

MORAG: Christie? It's Morag.

He opens his eyes. He tries to speak, but it comes out garbled.

I didn't come before now because... it was you who told me never to come back to this christly place.

CHRISTIE smiles. He lifts his hands. They shake. MORAG takes them in hers.

And it was you who warned me that if I made myself into a doormat, there'd be a christly host of folks only too willing to tread over me.

CHRISTIE laughs with a wheeze.

And it was you taught me to never say the word "sorry" because it was a bloody awful christly word.

CHRISTIE is laughing, and so is MORAG.

(*Laughter and tears.*) But I am sorry, Christie. I am sorry I never came before. I am.

His hand reaches out and grasps hers.

I want you to know…you've always been a father to me, Christie.

With all the effort he can muster:

CHRISTIE: Well…
I'm…
Blessed.

CHRISTIE closes his eyes. And the "Scots" company members gather. The shadows of soldiers return.

PIPER: And Christie Logan was a great tall man…

SCOTS
MORAG: With the voice of drums…

PIPER: And the heart of a child…

SCOTS
MORAG: And the strength of conviction.

MORAG: Rise now, Christie Logan. Rise and follow.

The piper plays.

And CHRISTIE LOGAN rises and follows the piper off.

***

MORAG at the typewriter.

JULES calls from off.

JULES: Pique, *allons-y*?

PIQUE: Ready.

PIQUE comes on with her backpack.

JULES enters with guitar case.

PIQUE sees MORAG.

Mom. Why don't you come west with us?

JULES: Yes! Family trip to Galloping Mountain!

MORAG: I'd love to, but...

PIQUE: When I was out west, I went to see the Tonnerre shack, Ma. There wasn't any sign there's ever been a fire. The grass is thick and high. And you can hear the river speaking to you. Like it has a voice.

PIQUETTE: That was me. Whispering in your ear.

PIQUE: And when I got to Galloping Mountain, all the Tonneres came to say hi.

They greet her warmly.

And Lazarus's grave is there. With a simple cross.

LAZARUS: Welcome, my grandchild.

PIQUE: They got a whole community up there. You'll feel right at home, I know it. We could even visit Christie's grave.

CHRISTIE: Finally, I could meet the wee one.

PIQUE: Come with us, please?

MORAG:	I'll visit sometime. I have to stay here on my island. If I leave it now, I'll never finish this christly book.
JULES:	Hey, I've been meaning to show you both something.

CHRISTIE is there. LAZARUS and he talk.

CHRISTIE:	Lazarus.
LAZARUS:	Christie.
JULES:	The only thing I got that belonged to Lazarus, and it's a thing that wasn't even really his.
LAZARUS:	Got anything for me this week, Christie?
CHRISTIE:	Found this inside the house.

JULES and CHRISTIE both reach into their pockets.

JULES:	When I came back from the war, the old man gave it to me for safekeeping.
LAZARUS/ PIQUE:	What is it?
CHRISTIE:	Scots pin.
JULES:	Brooch.
CHRISTIE:	From the old country.
LAZARUS/ PIQUE:	"My Hope Is Constant in Thee." What's that mean?
CHRISTIE:	An old saying.
MORAG:	How in hell did Lazarus come to have that?

JULES:	All he told me is, he traded his knife for it. Thought it might be worth something someday.
PIQUE:	Ma, what's wrong!

MORAG goes to find the knife.

CHRISTIE:	What's that ya got?
LAZARUS:	Old knife.
MORAG:	Is this…is this Lazarus's knife?
CHRISTIE:	What's on it?
JULES:	Well, I'll be.
LAZARUS/ JULES	"T." For Tonnerre.
JULES:	Probably been in the family for a long time.
LAZARUS:	I got enough knives.
MORAG:	Jules, Lazarus traded his knife for that brooch… to Christie Logan.
LAZARUS:	Fair trade?
CHRISTIE:	Fair trade.
JULES:	You're kidding.
PIQUE:	These things do *not* happen.
MORAG:	Oh yes, they do. Everything moves both ways.

MORAG and JULES give her the knife and the brooch.

LAZARUS:	See ya next week, Christie?

CHRISTIE: Maybe. I'm taking care of a young lass.

LAZARUS: How's that?

CHRISTIE: Parents died. Got no home.

LAZARUS: You gonna be a father, Christie Logan?

CHRISTIE: Stranger things have happened.

JULES: You okay — Piquette?

PIQUETTE: *(To MORAG.)* Piquette.

                She leaves.

PIQUE: Yeh. I guess I don't feel so split anymore.

                They pick up their stuff. Hugs.

MORAG: Be safe honey. And you too… *(Nails it.)* Jules.

JULES: You got it!

MORAG: Only took thirty years.

                He leaves.

                ***

                ROYLAND arrives, with a willow in his hand. He looks tired.

MORAG: Royland. Are you okay?

ROYLAND: Divining at Tim Mackie's place today.

MORAG: And?

ROYLAND: … Nothing.

                He stares at the willow.

                I knew. The moment I started.

MORAG: Oh, Royland…

ROYLAND: People often lose the gift when they get older.

MORAG: Anybody can have a temporary setback.

ROYLAND: *(Without sentiment.)* No. I had it for a long while, and now I don't. It's as simple as that.

MORAG: What'll you do?

ROYLAND: Well, I'm not going to starve. Plenty of fish in that river.

            He turns to go, but then:

MORAG: Royland. What you've done. There are wells. Water. Real, wet, water. There are people in this world, like me, we never know if our tricks ever work, whether they even matter.

ROYLAND: Is it necessary, what you do?

MORAG: To me, yes.

ROYLAND: Then it matters.

            He hands the divining branch to her. She places it on her desk.

                          ***

            The company gathers around MORAG. She sees them now — her entire life surrounding her.

            As MORAG types, JULES accompanies PIQUE on guitar.

PIQUE: *(Singing.)* "There's a valley holds my name, now I know
            In the tales they used to tell it seemed so low
            There's a valley way down there
            I used to dream like a prayer
            And my mothers, they lived there long ago.

LAZARUS: *(Singing, in French.) Cette montagne qui porte mon nom, près du ciel*

LAZARUS/
PIQUE/
PIQUETTE: *(Singing, in French.) Ces histoires fait paraitre cette montagne si haute*
Y'a un chemin d'montagne la haut.Je vais respirer son air si beau.
Et les voix en moi j'te dit,ne mourraient jamais.

    MORAG reads from what she's typed.

MORAG: In the shallows...
The water's clear with undulating lines of gold...
As the sand ripples receive the sun.
But farther out...
The water deepens and keeps its life from all sight.
And when you're in that place of darkness...

COMPANY: *(Singing.)* There's a valley holds my name.
There's a valley holds my name.
There's a valley holds my name.
There's a valley holds my name.

    CRISPIN has handed MORAG a copy of the novel — The Diviners.

MORAG: ...when you're in that place of darkness...
...all you can do is...
Look ahead into the past.
And back into the future.
Until there's silence.

    She slowly hands the novel to PIQUE.

    PIQUE receives it, as the great gift it is.

End of Play

Study Guide

The following study guide was prepared for the Stratford Festival's 2024 première production of The Diviners *and has been adapted for inclusion in this book with the kind permission of the Stratford Festival.*

The Study Guide for *The Diviners* was created in collaboration with the Office of Indigenous Relations, University of Waterloo, with contributions from Dr. Sorouja Moll, Jessica Rumboldt and Summer Bressette as well as additional programming consultation with Elder Liz Stevens, Elder Jean Becker, Jay Havens, Emma Rain Smith and Robin Stadelbauer.

GRADE RECOMMENDATION

Grade 9+

CONTENT ADVISORY

The play explores mature subject matter including colonialism, racism and discrimination. There are references to domestic and child abuse. It also includes drinking and sexual content.

SYNOPSIS

Novelist Morag Gunn, estranged from her only daughter, unable to write, struggling with the bottle, is adrift in a river of memories. Travelling from the present to the past to an imagined future, Morag's journey encompasses her personal struggle for freedom and expression as well as those of the Métis and First Nations peoples of Manitoba. Adapted from Margaret Laurence's classic Canadian novel.

CURRICULUM CONNECTIONS

- Global Competencies
  - ∞ Citizenship, Collaboration, Critical Thinking, Creativity, Metacognition, Self-Awareness

- Grade 9–12
  - ∞ First Nations, Métis and Inuit Studies
  - ∞ Indigenous Languages
  - ∞ The Arts
  - ∞ Canadian and World Studies
  - ∞ English
  - ∞ Technological Education

- Grade 11–12
  - ∞ Social Sciences and Humanities

- Post-Secondary
  - ∞ Suitable for courses in disciplines such as Arts, Canadian Studies, Cultural Studies, Creative Writing, Drama or Theatre, English, Fine Arts, First Nations, Métis and Inuit Studies, Gender Studies, History, Human Rights, Indigenous Studies, Religious Studies, Social Development Studies, and Teacher Education.

THEMES

- Ancestry and Generational Relationships
- Circles and Cycles
- Class and Rural and Urban Contexts
- Colonialism, Racism and Discrimination

- Family, Mothers and Daughters
- Feminism, Gender and Agency
- The Human Need for Connection
- Language, Story and Identity
- Loneliness and Isolation
- Love
- Memory and Trauma
- Métis Identity, Music and Culture
- The Power of Water and Nature, and How They Move Us
- The Relationship between Past, Present and Future
- Revelation and Reclamation
- Secrecy and Shame
- Self-Discovery and Acceptance
- Truth and Reconciliation
- Writing and Writers

DISCUSSION AND REFLECTION QUESTIONS

Before Reading the Play:

- What do you already know about Métis identity, music and culture? Where did you learn this? What else would you like to learn?
- In the play's prologue, a river is compared to a Métis sash. Using resources such as www.metismuseum.ca and others, learn about the origin story of the Métis sash. How might the symbolism of a river be connected to the sash?
- What is the role of memories? How do memories shape our experiences on a day-to-day basis?
- Why do our "roots" matter? In what ways do ancestry and intergenerational relationships influence people's sense of place, belonging and identity?

- What is your understanding of the relationship between past, present and future?

- In *The Truth About Stories: A Native Narrative*, Thomas King says: "The truth about stories is, that's all we are." What does this mean to you? Do you agree? Explain why or why not.

- Think about the recurring stories in your life. Do you believe that the stories you retell yourself or that you hear repeatedly about you shape your identity? Why or why not?

- Why might parents keep the truth from their children? Do you think it's ever okay for adults to keep secrets from children? Explain your thinking.

- How would you define "colonialism," "racism," and "discrimination"? In what ways do you expect these might be a part of this play?

- This play is an adaptation of Margaret Laurence's novel by the same title, which was published in 1974 and is a new retelling that is collaboratively created. In what ways does this respond to the 83rd Call to Action from the Truth and Reconciliation Commission? Why might it be important for Indigenous and non-Indigenous artists to work together on artistic projects? How could projects like this contribute to the reconciliation process?

- There have been repeated attempts to ban Margaret Laurence's original novel and to prevent young people from reading it in school. Do you think it is important that young people are able to make their own choices about what they want to read? Should books ever be banned? Explain your position.

- Reflect on your own experiences with coming-of-age stories. How do you expect this play to explore the journey from adolescence to adulthood?

After Reading the Play:

- Think about Morag's journey travelling from the present to the past to an imagined future. In what ways did this journey reflect her struggle for freedom and expression?

- At what point does Morag's journey illustrate the human need for connection?

- Morag could not write and was aimlessly lost in a river of memories. How did her memories impact her work as an artist?

- Margaret Laurence, the writer of the novel on which the play is based, and Morag Gunn, the protagonist, are not of Métis heritage. What implications might this have for Métis representation in this play? In this adaptation, what choices might the intercultural creative team have made to centre the Métis characters, culture and experiences?

- How does Morag's journey connect to the struggles for freedom and expression for the Métis and First Nations peoples in Manitoba?

- Revisit your definitions of "colonialism," "racism," and "discrimination." In what ways did *The Diviners* reveal the impact of these? Include examples from the play.

- Look up the definition for the word "diviners" and consider its multiple meanings. Thinking back on your experience of this play, how do these definitions connect? How does this convergence of meaning contribute to the play's themes?

- What do the characters learn about family and home? How do their feelings about this change from the beginning to the end of the play? Share examples to support your thinking.

- Why did Jules refuse to sing "God Save the King"? Consider the lyrics and history of the anthem.

- Throughout the play, we see that Morag and Pique are at a delicate place of transition in their relationship. What responsibility does Morag have to her daughter in helping her find answers? What, if anything, do you think each of these characters could have done differently in relation to one another?

- Are there any unintentional harms that might be caused through the production of this play? If so, what are they and what might be done to take care of the artists and audience members participating in the work?

EXERCISES

River Stories
Offered by Dr. Sorouja Moll

Objective: Students will explore their histories, personal narratives, communities and sense of belonging, culminating in the creation of a collaborative visual representation with the aim of deepening their understanding of community, empathy and the interplay between personal stories and collective identity.

Materials:
- The poem "I Come From" by Dean Atta
- "I Come From" or "I Am From" Poem Template
- Writing utensils and paper and/or computer access
- Student photos or drawings of themselves
- Large pieces of craft paper (approx. 4 ft.) cut into long, winding, curvy pieces ("river") – one per student
- Large, uneven craft paper circle ("bay")

Directions:

1. Invite students to create a short poem about where they come from using poet Dean Atta's "I Come From" as a point of inspiration. Invite students to use the poem template as a way of structuring/beginning their writing. (Before they begin writing, let them know they will be asked to share at least a few lines, so should be mindful of creating something they are comfortable sharing.)

2. Ask students to draw or share a photo of themselves that they would be willing to share.

3. Provide each student with their "river."

4. Invite them to write sections from their poem on their river. They may choose to add drawings as well.

5. Position the large paper bay in the centre of the space. Completed rivers will be attached as if flowing into the bay. The rivers can converge into the central paper bay from any side.

6. Invite students to paste their photos of themselves in the central bay.

7. Decide as a classroom community where you want to display your community river.

8. Invite students, as they wish, to share (parts of) their poems with one another.

Debriefing Questions:

*   How did creating your poem make you feel?
*   If you chose to do so, did anything surprise you or stand out to you while sharing your story with your classmates?
*   How did seeing and hearing everyone's stories impact you?
*   In what ways do you think sharing personal stories like these can help build a stronger sense of community in our classroom?

- Have you ever heard "all my relations"? What does this Indigenous worldview mean? How might it connect to how we think about family, where we come from and where we belong?

Possible Extensions:
Research Project

Have students delve deeper into the historical context and cultural communities of where they live by creating a digital, interactive piece. Students might explore factors such as political events, economic conditions, or cultural changes that influenced their community's history. Collecting images and pieces of text, students can present their research.

Creative Writing

Encourage students to expand on a specific event or aspect of their family story they are curious about and would be willing to share through a fictionalized narrative. This could involve imagining scenes or dialogue based on historical or personal details, offering a deeper exploration in the vein of *The Diviners*.

Exploring Christi Belcourt's *The Wisdom of the Universe*
Offered by Summer Bressette

Objective: Students will explore Christi Belcourt's painting, *The Wisdom of the Universe*, as a way to engage in new thinking about Métis culture and artistry.

Materials:

- Projector and speaker
- Internet access
- An image of *The Wisdom of the Universe*, such as the one available on www.ago.ca
- A knowledge of the "See, Think, Wonder" process, available on www.facinghistory.org.

- The YouTube documentary from Art Gallery of Ontario titled *Multisensory Moments: Christi Belcourt's Wisdom of the Universe*
- Writing utensils and/or computer access

Directions:

1. Begin with Christi Belcourt's painting projected on the wall. (Do not yet share the title of the painting.)

2. Lead students through the "See, Think, Wonder" strategy to guide students' analysis.

3. Then, ask students to identify as many plants and animals as they can in the piece.

4. Share that the piece depicts 220 species of plants and animals in Southwestern Ontario that are extinct or nearing extinction. Many of these are medicinal plants.

5. Share the title of the piece and ask students to reflect on and respond to the following in discussion as a class, in small groups or individually:

   ∞ Why do you think this piece be called *The Wisdom of the Universe*?

   ∞ What do you notice about the form and style of the painting?

   ∞ What do you notice about the amount of symmetry in the piece?

   ∞ How might the symmetry be reflective of the title of the painting and the intentions of the artist?

6. Share the video *Multisensory Moments: Christi Belcourt's Wisdom of the Universe*, which is about commissioning *The Wisdom of the Universe*.

   ∞ How did watching this video and learning about Christi Belcourt as a Métis artist confirm, challenge or provide new thinking about the painting and about Métis culture?

Debriefing Questions:

- In what ways does experiencing this painting prompt new thinking about your responsibility toward the universe? What might it look like to have empathy for plants and animals? How might empathy be a step toward reconciliation?

- In what ways did the title of the painting, along with the artist's intention, align with or challenge your initial impressions of the artwork?

Possible Extensions:
Nature Walk

Take a nature walk and see if you come across anything identifiable from the painting, researching which of these are medicinal plants and, if so, how they are used.

Revitalizing Flora and Fauna

It is not only people who have been displaced and harmed by colonialism. Take time to learn about other plant or animal species impacted by colonization, such as the pawpaw fruit. Discuss the broader implications of human actions on biodiversity and ecosystems.

Visual Art by Meryl McMaster

Conduct the same exercise as above with a Meryl McMaster photograph such as *Do You Remember Your Dreams*. McMaster's work is a key visual art inspiration for *The Diviners* creative team.

Becoming Better Treaty Partners: Relationships Between Indigenous and Settler Communities

Examine relationships between Indigenous and settler communities. For example, since the 2022 Russian invasion of Ukraine, we have seen incredible solidarity between Indigenous and Ukrainian communities, a symbol of which is the kokum scarves. What other stories about relationships between Indigenous and settler communities do you know or might you learn about? How might these stories influence settlers to become better treaty partners?

ADDITIONAL RESOURCES

- Clan Gunn; Scots Connection:
  https://www.scotsconnection.com/clan_crests/gunn.htm

- Colonialism and Its Impact (2016); The Canadian Research Institute for the Advancment of Women:
  https://www.criaw-icref.ca/wp-content/uploads/2021/04/Local-Women-Matter-3-Colonialism-and-its-impacts.pdf

- Gabriel Dumont Institute Virtual Museum of Métis Culture and History:
  https://www.metismuseum.ca/collections.php

- Language and Identity; Facing History & Ourselves Canada:
  https://www.facinghistory.org/en-ca/resource-library/language-identity

- Margaret Laurence: *The Canadian Encyclopedia*:
  https://www.thecanadianencyclopedia.ca/en/article/margaret-laurence

- Keating, William. *Narrative of an Expedition to the Source of St. Peter's River, Lake Winnepeck, Lake of the Woods & etc. in the year 1823.* 1824:
  https://www.loc.gov/item/rc01001607/

- King, Thomas. *The Truth About Stories: A Native Narrative.* (House of Anansi Press, 2003.)

- *Métis Culture & Traditions*; Rupertsland Institute:

https://www.rupertsland.org/wp-content/
uploads/2022/03/Metis-Culture-and-Traditions-
Foundational-Knowledge-Themes-01.25.22.pdf

- Troupe, Cheryl. *Expressing Our Heritage: Métis Artistic Designs*. (Gabriel Dumont Institute of Native Studies, 2002.)

Offered by Members of *The Diviners* Creative Team of Krista Jackson, Yvette Nolan, Geneviève Pelletier and Vern Thiessen

- Andrina Turenne, Musician and Composer for 2024 World Première of *The Diviners*: https://www.andrinaturenne.com

- Campbell, Maria. *Halfbreed*. (McClelland & Stewart, 2019.)

- Etchiboy: Métis Fashion: https://www.etchiboy.com/en/

- Iwama, Marilyn, et al. *Two-Eyed Seeing and the Language of Healing in Community-Based Research*, 2009: https://ojs.library.ubc.ca/index.php/CJNE/article/view/196493/191588

- Kostash, Myrna. *The Seven Oaks Reader*. (NeWest Press, 2016.)

- Laurence, Margaret. *Dance on the Earth: A Memoir.* (McClelland & Stewart, 1989.

- Laurence, Margaret.*The Diviners*. (McClelland & Stewart, 1974; Penguin Modern Classics, 2017.)

- *Margaret Laurence, First Lady of Manawaka*; National Film Board: https://www.nfb.ca/film/margaret_laurence_first_lady_of_manawaka/

- The Margaret Laurence Home; Neepawa Tourism: https://neepawatourism.ca/attractions/the-margaret-laurence-home/
  Margaret Laurence House; Provincial Heritage Sites, Manitoba Sport, Culture & Heritage: https://www.gov.mb.ca/chc/hrb/prov/p025.html

- "Margaret Laurence Writes the Diviners," CBC Interview: https://www.cbc.ca/player/play/audio/1.3627166

- Meryl McMaster, Visual Artist: http://merylmcmaster.com

- Métis Jig; Mikey Harris, TikTok: https://www.tiktok.com/@mikeyyharriss?lang=en

- Teillet, Jean. *The North-West is Our Mother: The Story of Louis Riel's People, the Métis Nation.* (HarperCollins, 2021.)

- Wente, Jesse. *Unreconciled: Family, Truth, and Indigenous Resistance.* (Penguin Random House Canada, 2022.)

- "The Women Behind the First Michif-French Dictionary," Kayla Rosen, CTV News: https://winnipeg.ctvnews.ca/the-women-behind-the-first-michif-french-dictionary-1.5009759?cache=mqtvfodkrwpz%3Fot%3DAjaxLayout

- World Virtual Indigenous Circle on Open Science and the Decolonization of Knowledge: https://www.unescochair-cbrsr.org/wp-content/uploads/2020/09/IndcircleWebinar_report_Final_01.pdf